THE BUSINESS OF LESS

The Business of Less rewrites the book on business and the environment.

For the last thirty years, corporate sustainability was synonymous with the pursuit of 'eco-efficiency' and 'win-win' opportunities. The notion of 'eco-efficiency' gives us the illusion that we can achieve environmental sustainability without having to question the pursuit of never-ending economic growth. The 'win-win' paradigm is meant to assure us that companies can be protectors of the environment while also being profit maximizers. It is abundantly clear that the state of the natural environment has further degraded instead of improved. This book introduces a new paradigm designed to finally reconcile business and the environment. It is called 'net green', which means that in these times of ecological overshoot, businesses need to reduce total environmental impact and not just improve the eco-efficiency of their products. The book also introduces and explains the four pollution prevention principles 'again', 'different', 'less', and 'labor, not materials'. Together, 'net green' and the four pollution prevention principles provide a road map, for businesses and for every household, to a world in which human prosperity and a healthy environment are no longer at odds.

The Business of Less is full of anecdotes and examples. This brings its material to life and makes the book not only very accessible but also hugely applicable for everyone who is worried about the fate of our planet and is looking for answers.

Roland Geyer is Professor of Industrial Ecology at the University of California, Santa Barbara. His work has been covered widely in the media, including worldwide appearances on radio and television shows. Learn more about Roland, his work, and its impact on www.rolandgeyer.com.

THE BUSINESS OF LESS

The Role of Companies and Households on a Planet in Peril

Roland Geyer

Routledge
Taylor & Francis Group

LONDON AND NEW YORK

First published 2022
by Routledge
2 Park Square, Milton Park, Abingdon, Oxon OX14 4RN

and by Routledge
605 Third Avenue, New York, NY 10158

Routledge is an imprint of the Taylor & Francis Group, an informa business

British Library Cataloguing-in-Publication Data
A catalogue record for this book is available from the British Library

Library of Congress Cataloging-in-Publication Data
Names: Geyer, Roland, author.
Title: The business of less : the role of companies and households on a
    planet in peril / Roland Geyer.
Description: First Edition. | New York : Routledge, 2021. | Includes
    bibliographical references and index. |
Identifiers: LCCN 2021010332 (print) | LCCN 2021010333 (ebook) | ISBN
    9780367755836 (hardback) | ISBN 9780367755850 (paperback) | ISBN
    9781003163060 (ebook)
Subjects: LCSH: Industrial management—Environmental aspects. | Business
    enterprises—Environmental aspects. | Social responsibility of business. |
    Environmental protection.
Classification: LCC HD30.255 .G49 2021 (print) | LCC HD30.255 (ebook) |
    DDC 658.4/08—dc23
LC record available at https://lccn.loc.gov/2021010332
LC ebook record available at https://lccn.loc.gov/2021010333

ISBN: 978-0-367-75583-6 (hbk)
ISBN: 978-0-367-75585-0 (pbk)
ISBN: 978-1-003-16306-0 (ebk)

DOI: 10.4324/9781003163060

Typeset in Joanna
by Apex CoVantage, LLC

The price of abundance is restraint.
Greg Critser, Fatland, 2003

For Lisa, Lorelei, and Orlando

CONTENTS

PREFACE

In 2016, I requested sabbatical leave with the intent to write a textbook on energy and the environment. Yet, when I settled down to pore over my data on energy consumption, conversion efficiencies, and greenhouse gas emissions, I realized that I had to write a different book. It is the one you are holding right now.

My journey towards this book began when I noticed the widening gap between the perpetual optimism of the corporate sustainability literature and the increasingly desperate-sounding reports about the state of the environment. If we were making all these amazing strides in corporate greening, why did the health of our planet go from bad to worse? It didn't make any sense, so I decided to get to the bottom of this seeming contradiction.

My somewhat unusual path may have helped me in this endeavor. After finishing a graduate degree in physics, I started a career in the financial industry. This experience was intellectually and financially rewarding but reinforced my desire to turn my passion for the environment into my profession. I acquired the necessary sustainability expertise at two very different places. One was INSEAD, a leading business school, and the other the interdisciplinary Centre for Environmental Strategy, which is housed within the engineering department of the University of Surrey. In 2003, I joined the faculty of UCSB's Bren School of Environmental Science and Management, where I am surrounded by environmental and social scientists. Twenty-three years of studying environmental sustainability, or the lack thereof, while being exposed to all these different disciplines and schools of thought has given me some unique insights. These are what I am going to share with you in this book.

Its structure started falling into place once I fully embraced the fact that I do not agree with some of the central tenets of the corporate sustainability literature. One of these is the assertion that we can achieve sustainability merely by focusing on reducing the environmental impact per product or service. This is called 'eco-efficiency'. The second paradigm is the belief that the prospect of increased revenues or profits is, and should be, the sole motive behind corporate environmental efforts. This is called 'win-win' or 'double dividends'. The first part of this book is a careful examination of these paradigms and their fundamental problems.

The second part of the book introduces a set of principles and strategies that will enable us finally to reconcile business and environmental sustainability. When I wrote this section, I soon realized that one cannot truly explore the lack of sustainability in our current production systems without thinking about the unsustainable ways in which we all currently consume. As a result, I ended up writing a book that is as relevant for households as it is for businesses. With this in mind, I have also ended the book with two summary chapters, one with a business perspective and the other with a household view.

While I wish I had written this book twenty years ago, I could not have done so. It has taken me until now to develop all the ideas it contains and also the confidence to publicly renounce the current corporate sustainability gospel. Doing the latter is not just immensely liberating but also absolutely necessary if we are to meaningfully explore and define the role of business and households on a planet in peril.

And a planet in peril it is. In the four short years it has taken me to complete this book, the state of the environment has deteriorated so much, I have had to rewrite Chapter 1 multiple times in order to keep up with the pace of its decline. In December 2019, I rented a beautiful off-grid cabin above Carmel Valley, CA, where I wrote Chapter 6. By summer 2020, the cabin had burned down in what turned out to be the worst fire season in California's history. As I write this preface, the annual count of western monarch butterflies wintering in California is coming to a close. Like all Californians, my family loves the monarchs, and our annual trip to a local eucalyptus grove teeming with butterflies has always been one of our favorite traditions. Yet, in the seventeen years we have been living here, their population has plunged from millions to fewer than two thousand. Where branches were once festooned with thousands of these beautiful creatures in the colder months, there are now only deserted trees. It may be too late to save the western monarch, but we have so much more to lose. I believe that there can be room for all species on this planet if we finally change the way we produce and consume. The purpose of this book is to show us how.

Roland Geyer
Santa Barbara, California, 8 February 2021

πάητα ρεῖ

ACKNOWLEDGMENTS

While writing a book is a somewhat solitary exercise, it would not have been possible without the help and support of an ever-growing number of people. I want to take this opportunity to thank at least some of them here.

I would like to express my deep gratitude to my mentors Roland Clift, Tim Jackson, Bob Ayres, and Luk van Wassenhove. Meeting and working with them truly changed my life.

I would like to thank my PhD students and PostDocs Vered Blass, Trevor Zink, Joe Palazzo, Jason Maier, Jessica Couture, Timnit Kefela, Eric Fournier, Brandon Kuczenski, Adriana Dominguez, and Huseyin Sarialtin. I loved and love working with every one of you.

At the Bren School, I get to interact daily with our amazing master's students, a significant number of whom turn into my colleagues and friends. I would like to single out Garrett Eyer, Ilan MacAdam-Somer, Jimi Kallaos, Ashley Henderson, Ian Creelman, Kevin Langham, Andy Bilich, and Cameron Gray, but the list could go on for much longer.

Next, I would like to say heartfelt thanks to all my colleagues and collaborators over the years, in particular David Stoms, Kara Lavender Law, Jenna Jambeck, Don Malen, Dick Startz, Bob Boughton, and Fred Chong.

Finally, I would like to give very special thanks to my wonderful wife, Lisa, for her unstinting support, advice, and encouragement, and to my beloved children, Lorelei and Orlando. It is my concern for their – and all children's – uncertain future which fuels everything I do.

1

WHY LESS?

In January 1991, Professor Roland Clift settled into his window seat and took in the view of Santa Barbara, California, nestled between the Santa Ynez Mountains and the Pacific Ocean below him. A conference called "The Emerging Pollution Prevention Paradigm" had just finished, and he was flying back to London, deep in thought. From high above, it looked like humankind and nature were in perfect harmony, but Professor Clift knew that the ground truth was different. It was nearly thirty years ago that Rachel Carson had published *Silent Spring* – the book that warned of the indiscriminate use of pesticides like DDT, helped start the modern environmental movement, and had the chemical industry up in arms. DDT was now banned in many countries, but as a chemical engineer, Professor Clift knew that DDT was only one of countless chlorinated organic compounds that were accumulating in the environment. As he looked out into the seemingly endless expanse of the Pacific Ocean, Clift knew that minor course corrections were not enough. He took a hearty sip of his gin and tonic and nodded to himself. Right there and then, Roland Clift decided to

DOI:10.4324/9781003163060-01

resign as head of the Chemical Engineering Department at the University of Surrey in the UK, establish the Centre for Environmental Strategy, and dedicate the rest of his career to the pursuit of sustainability. Once he was back in England, Professor Clift spent eighteen months finding the funds to start the Centre. By the time the Earth Summit in Rio de Janeiro was underway in June 1992, the Centre for Environmental Strategy was about to open for business. The timing could not have been better. In Rio, 172 governments, hundreds of non-governmental organizations (NGOs), and thousands of individuals came together to "rethink economic development and find ways to stop polluting the planet and depleting its natural resources."[1]

The Earth Summit was proof that environmentalism was finally leaving its niche existence and going mainstream. It also galvanized an overwhelming amount of governmental and corporate activity on environmental sustainability, including commissions, roundtables, councils, one-off reports, annual reports, environmental performance indicators, and sustainable development goals (simply called SDGs by the in-crowd). It even created entirely new professions, from green supply chain managers to chief sustainability officers. Within twenty years after Rio, the environment had turned from a penniless pursuit to a smart career move, from Greenpeace activism in Birkenstock sandals and hemp shirts to environmental accounting at PricewaterhouseCoopers (PwC) in Boss suits and Ralph Lauren ties. Each time I'm being complimented on my clever career choice, I have to stop myself from pointing out that when I made this choice it was anything but clever.

It is astonishing how much things have changed since Professor Clift quit his position in 1991. In the same year, a handful of idealists at the University of Stuttgart, who all shared a passion for a then obscure environmental analysis method called life cycle assessment (LCA), started a small consultancy. Less than twenty years later, neither LCA nor the consultancy were obscure anymore. In 2009, the Wall Street Journal even profiled one of their directors in an article titled 'Hot Job: Calculating Products' Pollution'.[2] In the same year, LCA was listed by Time Magazine as one of '10 Ideas Changing the World Right Now'.[3] Ten years after that, the consultancy was acquired by Sphera, a leading provider of integrated sustainability and risk management services. Many companies now have groups of in-house LCA experts themselves, and even more have sustainability staff. It is hard to find a multinational corporation that does not declare its deep commitment to environmental sustainability or an issue of The Economist or Harvard Business Review without an article on business and the environment.

Yet, despite the countless efforts and activities, humankind has not come any closer to living sustainably. On the contrary, things continue to get worse. Reading the Global Environmental Outlook (GEO) reports, published by the United Nations Environmental Program (UNEP), feels a bit like watching Groundhog Day. In 2012, the press release of GEO-5 was titled "World remains on unsustainable track despite hundreds of internationally agreed goals and objectives."[4] In 2019, the press release for GEO-6 read "damage to the planet is so dire that people's health will be increasingly threatened unless urgent action is taken."[5] Here are some of the headlines describing the state of the environment in GEO-6: *A major species extinction event is unfolding. Ecosystem integrity and functions are declining. Coral reefs are being devastated. Land degradation and desertification have increased. In most regions, freshwater quality has worsened significantly since 1990. Consumption rates and linear activities (extract-make-use-dispose) have increased resource exploitation beyond the recovery ability of ecological systems. The food system is increasing pressure on local ecosystems and the global climate.* I'll stop here. You get the idea. Since the signing of the Rio Declaration, the Agenda 21, the Forest Principles, and the Conventions on Climate Change and Biodiversity in 1992, glaciers and remnant forests have been disappearing at increasing speeds, while biodiversity and animal populations have been declining rapidly. We are clearly better at passing declarations and resolutions than implementing them. This is particularly true when it comes to climate change.

Anthropogenic climate change is generated when human-caused emissions into air absorb the infrared radiation from the earth and radiate part of it right back at it, thus disturbing the radiation balance of our planet. This heat-trapping mechanism is called greenhouse effect, and the emissions that cause it are called greenhouse gases (GHGs). The most important anthropogenic GHG is carbon dioxide (CO_2), which is released when fossil fuels are burned, certain industrial processes are run, or when land is deforested or otherwise degraded. International negotiations with the aim to combat anthropogenic climate change led to the Kyoto Protocol in 1997. Let history be the judge of whether the Kyoto Protocol was a political failure or not, but so far it certainly failed to reduce global GHG emissions. In its successor, the 2015 Paris Agreement, 195 national governments agreed to the "long-term goal of keeping global average temperature to well below 2°C above pre-industrial levels" and "to aim to limit the increase to 1.5°C."

Climate data suggest that it might be too late for these goals already. According to the National Oceanic and Atmospheric Administration

(NOAA) of the U.S. Department of Commerce, 2014–2020 were the seven warmest years since recordkeeping began, and global average temperature appears to have reached 1°C above pre-industrial levels already.[6] Global annual mean atmospheric CO_2 concentration now exceeds 410 parts per million (ppm).[7] Atmospheric CO_2 concentration is the single most important indicator for monitoring anthropogenic climate change. Its pre-industrial level was 280 ppm, and according to ice core measurements, it has not exceeded 300 ppm during the last 800,000 years.[8]

Four years have passed since the initial draft of this chapter, so I keep having to update it with more bad news. It is now January 2021, exactly thirty years after Roland Clift's fateful flight, and I am writing this final version at my desk at the University of California, Santa Barbara, with the Pacific Ocean visible through my office window on the left. California is trying to recover from the worst fire season it ever had; so is Australia.[9] The American Southwest is in the iron grip of a persistent drought, but so is Germany.[10] The year 2020 may be remembered as the year that climate change finally became an undeniable reality for most.

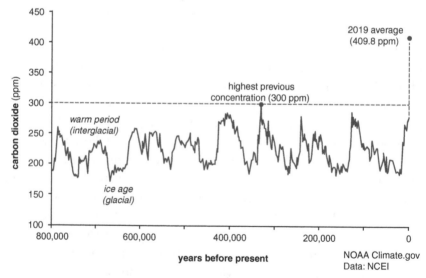

Figure 1.1 Atmospheric CO_2 concentration

Source: (Image source: NOAA)[11]

How can this dismal environmental record since the Rio Conference be reconciled with all the governmental and corporate sustainability efforts mentioned earlier? The short answer is growth. According to the World Bank, global gross domestic product (GDP) has more than doubled between 1992 and 2019, from 39 to 85 trillion 2010 USD.[12] Be aware that for comparability all GDP values in this book are given in constant 2010 USD, since we want to compare the purchasing power of GDP not their nominal values. The nominal values get much smaller as you go back in time, since in 1962 one dollar bought much more than one dollar in 1992 and even more than one dollar today. For example, in 1962 the price of a McDonald's hamburger was 15 cents. But back to the growth in global GDP. So, adjusted for inflation, the economic value of all goods and services produced annually today is over twice as much as it was in 1992. Let's pause for a minute to take this in.

At the beginning of the 1990s, the United Nations (UN) became so worried about humankind's trajectory that, in their own words, "the UN sought to help Governments rethink economic development and find ways to halt the destruction of irreplaceable natural resources and pollution of the planet."[13] There were good reasons for this sentiment. The thirty years since *Silent Spring* was published in 1962 had seen phenomenal economic growth, and the environmental consequences were impossible to ignore. In 1962, global GDP (in constant 2010 USD) was 13 trillion. In the thirty years between 1962 and 1992, it had thus tripled to 39 trillion. While the social benefits of this growth were undeniable, they were also distributed very unevenly. More importantly for this book, such enormous economic growth had created enormous environmental pressures. 'Rethinking economic development' seemed indeed called for.

By everyone's account the Rio Conference was a huge wake-up call and a tremendous success. An entire encyclopedia could be filled with the governmental and corporate sustainability activities that have been undertaken and commitments that have been made since. Yet today, nearly thirty years after Rio, the world also produces goods and services every year that have well over twice the economic value of all goods and services provided during the year the Earth Summit took place. So, in tandem with all our environmental sustainability efforts we more than doubled annual economic output. This may have been a great thing for producers and consumers alike, but it was unlikely to be good news for the environment, which was already deemed in peril nearly thirty years ago.

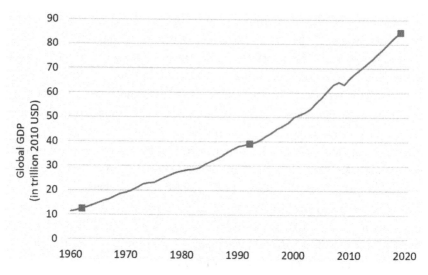

Figure 1.2 Global gross domestic product (GDP)[14]

One positive development worth pointing out at this point is that the environmental impact per unit of GDP has been decreasing, at least for a number of important environmental indicators. This phenomenon is known as 'decoupling' between environmental impact and economic output. For example, the carbon intensity of the global economy, measured in grams of CO_2 emitted per dollar GDP produced has decreased considerably since 1992, from 560 to 420 grams of CO_2 per 2010 USD.[15] Just seen on its own, this is a success story; a prime example and show case of decoupling. But by now you are probably already multiplying the carbon intensities of economic output with the global GDP numbers from the previous section in order to obtain global annual CO_2 emissions.

I'm afraid your calculations are correct; between 1992 and 2019, global CO_2 emissions went from 22 to 36 billion metric tons per year. With the global economy more than doubling in size, reducing its carbon intensity by 25% is nowhere near enough to arrest the growth of global CO_2 emissions. And total emissions, not emissions per dollar of economic output, is the metric that matters for the stability of the global climate, since even the 1992 CO_2 emission level was already unsustainable. In fact, according to the Intergovernmental Panel on Climate Change of the United Nations,

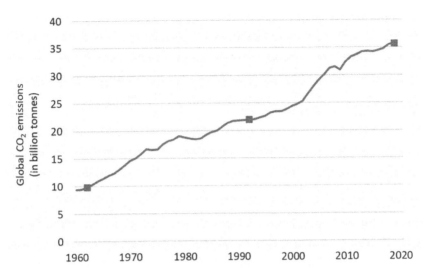

Figure 1.3 Global CO$_2$ emissions from fossil fuel combustion and cement production[16]

limiting warming to 1.5°C would require global net human-caused CO$_2$ emissions to fall roughly 45% from 2010 levels by 2030 and reach net zero around 2050.[17]

The carbon intensity of GDP is just one example of measuring the 'eco-efficiency' of economic activity or output. In an introduction to eco-efficiency, the World Business Council on Sustainable Development (WBCSD), which is a big supporter of the concept, points out that it basically means 'doing more with less'. WBCSD further explains that eco-efficiency "creates more value with less impact by unlinking goods and services from the use of nature."[18] This idea, which is extremely popular in the world of corporate environmental sustainability, has many different names and has generated reams of literature. Just try the following terms in a library or internet search engine: Energy efficiency, resource efficiency, resource productivity, decarbonization, dematerialization, and of course, the aforementioned decoupling. You can even find publications that delineate eco-efficiency from eco-effectiveness or ponder upon the difference between resource efficiency and resource productivity (spoiler alert: One is the reciprocal of the other). What all of these notions have in common is that quantitative measures of them consist of a ratio between an environmental and an economic indicator. The economic indicator typically measures economic value in one way or another, such as GDP. The environmental indicator can be a myriad of things, such as grams of CO_2 emitted, the climate change/acidification/eutrophication/toxicity/ etc. potential of substances released or emitted, megajoules of energy used, kilograms of materials used, kilograms of waste generated, and so on. There are at least three reasons behind the immense appeal of eco-efficiency approaches. One is that promoting efficiency is an easy sell since efficiency is a near-universal virtue. Who would dare to argue against it? Who wouldn't like to be more efficient? The second reason is that 'doing more with less' sounds like good business, too. Says the WBCSD about eco-efficiency: "Not only can it save production costs but can also open up new sources of revenue for companies."[19] The third reason is that the most effective conversation killer in any corporate environmental sustainability gathering is to question the need for growth. The necessity of growth is so taken for granted that many prefer to talk about sustainable growth rather than sustainable development. The seemingly hard-wired growth imperative is probably the reason why an influential book published in 1998 in support of resource productivity, Factor Four by Weizsäcker, Lovins & Lovins, is subtitled Doubling Wealth, Halving Resource Use, rather than 'doing the same with four times less'. It subtly suggests that we can have our cake and eat it, too. Talking about resource productivity and cake, I can't help thinking of a sketch in the BBC comedy show Little Britain. Marjorie Dawes, the fictional representative of the fictional weight-loss program FatFighters, who is as rude as she is upbeat, gives her group a brilliant piece of advice regarding her Half the Calories Diet: "If you take a bit of cake and cut it in half, then it's only half the calories. And because it's only half the calories, you can have twice as much." Well, we certainly doubled GDP (which is not the same as wealth as Factor Four carefully points out towards the end of the book). But what about resource use?

Measuring resource use is not straightforward, since it depends, among other things, on the types of material or resource flows to be included. According to the GEO-5 assessment, one silver lining was that, just like carbon intensity, the materials intensity of GDP had been decreasing between 1992 and 2007.[20] Unfortunately, a more recent UNEP report called Global Material Flows and Resource Productivity comes to the conclusion that the materials intensity of the world economy has been increasing since 2000.[21] It is not entirely clear whether it is worthwhile to settle this apparent disagreement, since no one questions that total use of materials or resources has been growing more or less continuously during the nearly thirty years since the Earth Summit. Materials or resource intensity may or may not have gone down, but total use, which is what truly matters, certainly went up. In fact, in 2020, the total mass of all human-made materials started to exceed all living biomass on Earth.[22]

To bring the slightly abstract issue of resource use to life, let's consider the five most widely used structural materials: Wood, concrete, steel, plastic, and aluminum. Just like carbon, oxygen, hydrogen, nitrogen, and phosphorus are the key nutrients in the natural world; wood, concrete, steel, plastic, and aluminum are the key nutrients of the industrial world, which would be unthinkable without them. Just look around you and out of your window, and consider the materials that the things you see are made of. What would it look like if you took those five materials away? Of those five, wood is the odd one out, since it has been used since time immemorial and also because it is a so-called renewable resource. Renewable here means that we can grow more trees if we need more wood, which does not imply that using wood has no environmental impact. The other four materials are man-made and were not produced or used in large quantities prior to the industrial revolution. Modern concrete, which is a mix of aggregate, water, and so-called hydraulic cement, was not common until well into the 19th century. Hydraulic cement, by far the most important of which is called Portland cement, chemically reacts with water which solidifies the mixture; the aggregate provides volume. Modern steel making only began after the invention of the Bessemer process in 1855, which enabled inexpensive removal of excess carbon and impurities. Think of steel as iron with a finely adjusted carbon content and some other alloying elements. Aluminum was only discovered in 1825 and originally more expensive than gold. The Bayer and Hall-Héroult processes, which finally enabled affordable mass production of aluminum, were invented in 1888 and 1886. Like steel, most aluminum grades also contain alloying elements. Synthetic plastic is the youngest of the five materials, and mass production only started after the Second World War. Plastic is a summary term for a wide range of synthetic organic polymers. Most plastics also contain chemical additives to enhance their properties.

Materials are so important to humankind that we name historical periods after them. As Michael Ashby says in his book *Materials Selection in Mechanical Design*: "Throughout history, materials have limited design."[23] New materials can offer new possibilities, which is exciting. New materials may also simply offer technical or cost advantages relative to the incumbent materials. As a result, material selection changes over time. Ashby illustrates this with the example of the vacuum cleaner, which started to gain popularity around 1900. Over the course of the 20th century, the dominant material of vacuum cleaners changed from wood to steel in the 1950s and finally plastic in the 1980s. This transition from wood to steel to plastic is apparent in many other household items, be it toys, tools, or appliances. Another example is food and beverage packaging, which used to be done almost exclusively with glass and steel but is now dominated by plastic and also aluminum. After the invention of the automobile, steel soon took over from wood as the main structural material. Today, steel is being challenged by so-called light-weight materials, such as aluminum and fiber-reinforced polymers. Light-weight automotive materials are an interesting case since they are marketed, at least in part, based on environmental performance. Light-weight materials enable automotive engineers to reduce the mass of cars without having to reduce their size (Can you hear Marjorie Dawes? Sounds a bit like having your cake and eating it, too). Mass reduction improves the fuel economy of the car and thus reduces tail-pipe emissions per vehicle mile driven (another eco-efficiency measure). As structural automotive material, aluminum actually has a cost disadvantage and some technical challenges relative to steel, so the aluminum industry also uses environmental arguments to market aluminum as a desirable structural automotive material. This is not an outlier. Increasingly, environmental performance is a third dimension of materials competition, in addition to cost and technical performance. Today, companies and industry associations spend significant time, effort, and money to assess which material has a better environmental performance in a given application. In principal, this should be good news, since it raises the possibility that the use of environmentally superior materials increases at the expense of more impactful ones.

So, let's take a moment to look at how global production and use of wood, cement, steel, aluminum, and plastic have changed since the Rio Conference in 1992. Figure 1.4 shows annual production normalized to

1992. The sobering results are even more dramatic than the global development of GDP. Between 1992 and 2019,

- annual global industrial roundwood production increased by 34%,
- annual global hydraulic cement production increased by a factor of 3.3,
- annual global crude steel production increased by a factor of 2.6,
- annual global primary aluminum production increased by a factor of 3.3,
- and annual global synthetic polymer production increased by a factor of 3.3.

The outlier is global wood production, which only grew by a modest 34%. As far as the four man-made materials are concerned, we did not, like Factor Four encouraged us, halve resource use; we doubled or tripled it instead. In other words, competition between the materials did not create a materials version of what the economist Schumpeter called creative destruction, the new replacing the old, a winner outcompeting a loser. We are not using steel and concrete instead of wood or plastic and aluminum instead of steel.

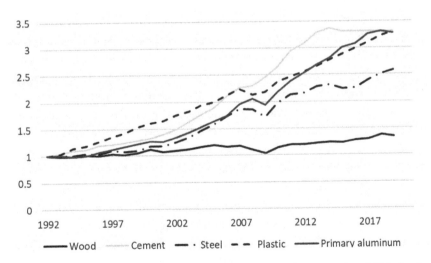

Figure 1.4 Global production of our main structural materials. 1992 levels: hydraulic cement 1,241, crude steel 723, synthetic polymers 141, primary aluminum 19 (all in million metric tons); industrial roundwood 1.51 billion cubic meters[24]

We use them in addition. There appear to be only winners in materials competition. The only loser, again, appears to be the environment. Just to keep the annual environmental impact from cement, steel, plastic, and aluminum production constant since the Earth Summit, impact per ton of material would have had to go down by 60–70%. And remember, 1992 was the year the UN implored the world's governments to "find ways to halt the destruction of irreplaceable natural resources and pollution of the planet."

By the way, the Rio Conference was not the first time that it was suggested that unfettered growth is likely to have severe environmental implications. In 1972, ten years after Silent Spring, another seminal book was published called Limits to Growth.[25] It reported the findings from a major computer simulation of the world in which the economy and the population grow exponentially but the natural environment is finite. Today, PhD students can run such simulations on their laptops, but back in 1972 this was a big deal. The findings of the simulations were dire, and, unsurprisingly, the book was criticized sharply. But then postulating that business as usual would lead to global 'overshoot and collapse' is unlikely to make you popular. At least some of the criticism was simply based on misunderstandings of the model. One was the focus on the availability of non-renewable natural resources, which is just one of the planetary limits of the model; the other limit is the use of the natural environment as a sink of pollution. It frequently went unnoted that the dire predictions did not substantially change when the model assumed an infinite amount of natural resources. The model was also misunderstood as generating precise forecasts rather than plausible scenarios. Today, after decades of experience with complex computer simulations with major uncertainties, such as climate models, it is common wisdom that they generate ranges of likely scenarios rather than a singular prediction. Today, it is also increasingly accepted that using the environment as a sink of pollution is the constraint that will bite long before we run out of natural resources. For example, we will have wrecked the climate long before we run out of fossil fuels. One final error regarding Limits to Growth is the mistaken believe that history proved it wrong a long time ago. The standard scenario of the world model in Limits to Growth finds that global population would peak right around 2050 and decline sharply thereafter. So, history has not yet falsified this grim prediction.

The story is the same wherever we look. Despite a lot of sustainability talk and plenty of good faith effort, total environmental impact continues to increase year over year. Yes, there is no shortage of eco-efficiency success stories. But somehow, they fail to translate into actual reduction of environmental impact, which is what is urgently needed and has been urgently needed for the last thirty years and more. By now this has turned into a Herculean task. It will take every willing individual, every willing stakeholder from all walks of life and parts of society to finally move the needle. But there is no doubt in my mind that it cannot be done without business. By business I mean everyone, from the baker down the street to the global corporation with billions of dollars in annual revenues. Businesses – big and small – make, move, and market the products we use every day. Businesses provide employment, income, and meaning. Businesses are simply how most of humankind organizes itself. But business as usual is not an option. Well, it is, but then we'll face the consequences, and they will be dire, as GEO-6 points out. We need business, but we need a different kind of business. We need business that reduces environmental impact. We need the business of less.

Notes

1 "Conferences, Environment and Sustainable Development," *United Nations*, accessed February 1, 2021, www.un.org/en/conferences/environment.

2 Ana Campoy, "Hot Job: Calculating Products' Pollution," *Wall Street Journal*, last modified September 1, 2009, accessed July 21, 2020, www.wsj.com/articles/SB125176415696374409.

3 Bryan Walsh, "10 Ideas Changing the World Right Now: Ecological Intelligence," *TIME Magazine*, March 12, 2009, accessed February 1, 2021, http://content.time.com/time/specials/packages/article/0,28804,1884779_1884782_1884776,00.html.

4 United Nations Environment Programme (UNEP), "Global Environment Outlook 5: Environment for the Future We Want," *UNEP*, (2012), accessed July 21, 2020, www.unenvironment.org/resources/global-environment-outlook-5.

5 United Nations Environment Programme (UNEP), "Global Environment Outlook 6: Healthy Planet Healthy People," *UNEP*, (2019), accessed July 21, 2020, www.unenvironment.org/resources/global-environment-outlook-6.

6   National Centers for Environmental Information, "Global Climate Report –
     Annual 2020," *National Oceanic and Atmospheric Administration*, (2020),
     accessed January 27, 2021, www.ncdc.noaa.gov/sotc/global/202013.

7   Global Monitoring Laboratory – Earth System Research Laboratories,
     "Trends in Atmospheric Carbon Dioxide," *National Oceanic and Atmospheric
     Administration*, accessed January 27, 2021, www.esrl.noaa.gov/gmd/ccgg/
     trends/gl_data.html.

8   Dieter Lüthi et al., "High-Resolution Carbon Dioxide Concentration Record
     650,000–800,000 Years Before Present," *Nature* 453 (2008): pp. 379–
     382, accessed February 2, 2021, https://doi.org/10.1038/nature06949.

9   "California's Wildfire Hell: How 2020 Became the State's Worst Ever
     Fire Season," *The Guardian*, last modified December 30, 2020, accessed
     January 27, 2021, www.theguardian.com/us-news/2020/dec/30/california-
     wildfires-north-complex-record; Jamie Tarabay, "Why These Australia
     Fires Are Like Nothing We've Seen Before," *New York Times*, last modified
     January 21, 2020, accessed August 26, 2020, www.nytimes.com/2020/
     01/21/world/australia/fires-size-climate.html.

10   Park Williams et al., "Large Contribution from Anthropogenic Warming
     to An Emerging North American Megadrought," *Science* 368, no. 6488
     (April 2020): pp. 314–318, https://science.sciencemag.org/content/368/
     6488/314; Christoph Seidler, "Die verborgene Dürre," *Der Spiegel*, last
     modified December 20, 2020, accessed January 27, 2021, www.spiegel.
     de/wissenschaft/natur/duerre-boden-in-deutschland-leidet-unter-
     regenmangel-a-9fa6df06-11b9-4bc4-8ae3-54a8edb52096.

11   Global Monitoring Laboratory – Earth System Research Laboratories,
     "Trends in Atmospheric Carbon Dioxide," *National Oceanic and
     Atmospheric Administration*, accessed January 27, 2021, www.esrl.noaa.
     gov/gmd/ccgg/trends/gl_data.html.

12   "GDP (Constant 2010 USD)," *The World Bank*, accessed July 21, 2020,
     https://data.worldbank.org/indicator/NY.GDP.MKTP.KD?end=2019&start
     =1960&view=chart.

13   "Conferences, Environment and Sustainable Development," *United
     Nations*, accessed February 1, 2021, www.un.org/en/conferences/
     environment.

14   "GDP (Constant 2010 USD)," *The World Bank*, accessed July 21, 2020,
     https://data.worldbank.org/indicator/NY.GDP.MKTP.KD?end=2019&start
     =1960&view=chart.

15   Own calculations based on GDP data from the World Bank, and CO2 data from BP and CICERO. See also Figure 6 in Chapter 4. "Statistical Review of World Energy 2020," *British Petroleum*, (2020), accessed January 13, 2021, www.bp.com/en/global/corporate/energy-economics/statistical-review-of-world-energy.html; Robbie M. Andrew, "Global CO2 Emissions from Cement Production, 1928–2018," *CICERO Center for International Climate Research*, (2019), accessed January 13, 2021, https://essd.copernicus.org/preprints/essd-2019-152/essd-2019-152.pdf; "GDP (Constant 2010 USD)," *The World Bank*, accessed July 21, 2020, https://data.worldbank.org/indicator/NY.GDP.MKTP.KD?end=2019&start=1960&view=chart.

16   "Statistical Review of World Energy 2020," *British Petroleum*, (2020), accessed January 13, 2021, www.bp.com/en/global/corporate/energy-economics/statistical-review-of-world-energy.html; Robbie M. Andrew, "Global CO2 Emissions from Cement Production, 1928–2018," *CICERO Center for International Climate Research*, (2019), accessed January 13, 2021, https://essd.copernicus.org/preprints/essd-2019-152/essd-2019-152.pdf.

17   "Special Report: Global Warming of 1.5 °C," *Intergovernmental Panel on Climate Change*, accessed January 30, 2021, www.ipcc.ch/sr15/.

18   Katherine Madden, Rebekah Young, Kevin Brady, and Jennifer Hall, "Eco-efficiency Learning Module," *The World Business Council on Sustainable Development*, last modified August 24, 2006, accessed July 21, 2020, www.wbcsd.org/Projects/Education/Resources/Eco-efficiency-Learning-Module.

19   Katherine Madden, Rebekah Young, Kevin Brady, and Jennifer Hall, "Eco-efficiency Learning Module," *The World Business Council on Sustainable Development*, last modified August 24, 2006, accessed July 21, 2020, www.wbcsd.org/Projects/Education/Resources/Eco-efficiency-Learning-Module.

20   United Nations Environment Programme (UNEP), "Global Environment Outlook 5: Environment for the Future We Want," *UNEP*, (2012), accessed July 21, 2020, www.unenvironment.org/resources/global-environment-outlook-5.

21   United Nations Environment Programme (UNEP), "Global Material Flows and Resource Productivity: Assessment Report for the UNEP International Resource Panel," *UNEP*, (2016), accessed July 21, 2020, www.unenvironment.org/resources/report/global-material-flows-and-resource-productivity-assessment-report-unep.

22   Emily Elhacham et al., "Global Human-Made Mass Exceeds All Living Biomass," *Nature* 588 (2020): pp. 442–444, accessed February 1, 2021, https://doi.org/10.1038/s41586-020-3010-5.

23   Michael F. Ashby, *Materials Selection in Mechanical Design*, 5th ed. (Oxford: Butterworth-Heinemann, 2016).

24   "Forestry Production and Trade," *Food and Agriculture Organization of the United Nations*, accessed February 1, 2021, www.fao.org/faostat/en/#data/FO;

       "Cement Statistics and Information," *United States Geological Survey*, accessed February 1, 2021, www.usgs.gov/centers/nmic/cement-statistics-and-information; "Statistical Reports," *World Steel Association*, accessed February 1, 2021, www.worldsteel.org/steel-by-topic/statistics/steel-statistical-yearbook.html; "Primary Aluminium Production," *International Aluminium Institute*, accessed February 1, 2021, www.world-aluminium.org/statistics/primary-aluminium-production/#data; Roland Geyer, Jenna R. Jambeck, and Kara Lavender Law, "Production, Use, and Fate of All Plastics Ever Made," *Science Advances* 3, no. 7 (2017): e1700782, accessed February 1, 2021, https://advances.sciencemag.org/content/3/7/e1700782.

25   Donella H. Meadows, Dennis L. Meadows, Jorgen Randers, and William W. Behrens, *The Limits to Growth; A Report for the Club of Rome's Project on the Predicament of Mankind* (New York: Universe Books, 1972).

2

A BRIEF HISTORY OF BUSINESS
AND THE ENVIRONMENT

Today, business and the environment is no longer regarded as an irreconcilable dichotomy. Every year, countless MBA and other students learn to address corporate environmental sustainability challenges and diligently work through case studies like the following:

Talia Ibargüen, the newly appointed chief sustainability officer of Hops Inc., the world's leading provider of premium hops, looked up from her handcrafted reclaimed-wood desk and out of the window of her corner office towards the long rows of Cascade, Centennial, and Simcoe plants in the middle distance. It was Wednesday, September 28, 2016, and Ibargüen had just two more days to develop the new Sustainability Road Map that CEO Boadicea Hallertau had requested. Ibargüen was still unsure which key environmental performance indicators (KEPIs) to propose to best reflect Hops Inc.'s new Win-Win-Win Mission Statement. Thanks to the craft beer explosion, times were good for premium hop growers, but with the incredible growth in sales came increased scrutiny by environmental NGOs. Only last week the Rainforest Alliance had published photos that were supposedly

DOI:10.4324/9781003163060-02

showing illegal clear-cutting of Brazilian rainforest for new hop plantations. Ibargüen looked back at the pictures on her desk and wondered how best to reconcile Hallertau's ambitious plans for expansion with this new wave of reputational risks. This morning she had even seen a full-page ad in the New York Times *by PETA, demanding that only cage-free hops be used for beer brewing.*

Readers of Harvard Business School cases will instantly recognize the tone and style, even though I freely admit that this is a fictionalized and slightly tongue-in-cheek portrait of one of my many talented and inspiring ex-students.

Today, most MBA curricula seem to cover at least some aspects of corporate social responsibility. Business schools now offer courses with titles such as Corporate Environmental Management and Strategy, Business Strategies for Environmental Sustainability, Sustainable Finance, Green Marketing, or Environmentally Sustainable Supply Chains. This embrace of sustainability by business schools and growing parts of the business community is a fairly new development and started right around the time the Earth Summit took place. Right until then, the relationship between environmentalists and corporations was marked by confrontation and mutual distrust, not synergies and win-win opportunities. This chapter will take a moment to review the history of business and the environment. This will help us to better understand where we are today and where we need to go from here.

Humankind was certainly not without impact on its environment before the industrial revolution. The deforestation of the Mediterranean Basin during the Roman Empire is just one pertinent example.[1] However, the rapid growth in population and economic activity spurred by the new technologies of the 18th and 19th century led to an equally rapid increase in the scale and scope of environmental impacts. In the early 20th century, the next wave of industrialization began when factories exchanged steam engines with much more efficient electric motors. The subsequent invention of assembly lines took mass production to a whole new level. Nothing epitomizes this new mass production of consumer goods like Henry Ford's Model T. Between 1908 and 1927, over 15 million models were produced worldwide.[2]

The automobile, as it was then called, is not only an icon of the 20th century but also provides many excellent examples of the changing relationship between business and the environment. The beginnings of the first environmental drama surrounding the car takes us to the lab of the General Motors (GM) Research Corporation in Dayton, Ohio. There, on December 9, 1921, chemist Thomas Midgley and lab director Charles Kettering found out that tetraethyl lead (TEL) had excellent antiknock properties.[3] TEL itself had been discovered sixty-seven years earlier but was still unused due to its high toxicity. GM, at this point controlled by the Du Pont family and run by Alfred Sloan, was still urgently looking for a gasoline additive to reduce engine knock and increase octane rating. The former happens when the fuel/air mixture ignites too early; the latter boosts the power and efficiency of the engine. It was known to the central decision makers in this drama that ethanol was also an excellent antiknock and octane booster. Compared to TEL, however, it had several business disadvantages. Ethanol, unlike TEL, was extremely easy to produce, could not be patented, and the oil industry saw it as unwelcome competition, since it was also a viable alternative to gasoline. By 1923, GM and Standard Oil of New Jersey (Esso) owned patents related to TEL and formed the Ethyl Corporation to manufacture and market it. They hired DuPont to run the manufacturing plants. The shareholders of GM, Standard Oil of New Jersey (which later became Exxon), and DuPont were poised to make enormous amounts of money.

Unfortunately, the proposal to use TEL as gasoline additive almost instantly caused public health concerns. Acute lead poisoning was common in the early days of TEL production and drew scrutiny and plant closures by local governments. In 1923, medical and public health experts also started to warn that burning leaded gasoline in millions of cars would lead to chronic lead exposure. The affected corporations responded by attempting to control public and government opinion on the health risks of TEL as well as the medical and public health research. For the next forty-five years GM, Du Pont, and Standard Oil would successfully thwart any attempt to regulate leaded gasoline. Critically important was Robert Kehoe, a prominent public health scientist at the University of Cincinnati and the chief medical advisor to the Ethyl Corporation. Kehoe publicly stated that the Ethyl Corporation would stop the distribution of leaded gasoline if it turned out that it endangered the public. He is also credited with the introduction of what is known as the 'Kehoe Paradigm': In order to regulate a substance of public health concern, irrefutable proof of its adverse effects is required.

So, the burden of proof lies with the regulators. This is essentially the opposite of the so-called precautionary principle, which argues that it's better to be safe than sorry. It took four decades before Clair Patterson and others were able to provide that irrefutable proof[4] and another three until leaded gasoline was finally banned. By then, TEL had already caused catastrophic levels of global lead pollution.

The story of leaded gasoline is singular in some ways but quite common in others. Physics and chemistry saw incredible advances in the second half of the 19th and the first half of the 20th century. Mechanical and chemical engineers wasted no time translating them into awe-inspiring technologies, materials, and devices. Business schools started to appear, turning out leagues of graduates versed in the new 'science of management'. Mass production went hand in hand with mass distribution and consumption, and thus the modern linear supply chain came into being. These supply chains took in ever-growing amounts of raw materials and delivered an ever-increasing number and variety of products. Yet due to the ironclad laws of thermodynamics, this also generated ever-growing amounts of wastes and emissions during the production, use, and eventual disposal of all these new goods. The earth still seemed so vast that early warnings that we might eventually overuse its natural resources or overrun its capacity to assimilate our wastes and emissions sounded ludicrous to almost everyone.

It took a long procession of incidents and disasters to convince a critical mass of government officials and the public at large that action was urgently required to mitigate the environmental impacts from industrial production and consumption.

Here are just a few highlights: From 1942 to 1953, the Hooker Electrochemical Company dumped its toxic chemical waste into the so-called Love Canal in Niagara Falls, NY. After it was closed and covered, the former dump site became a low-income housing development, complete with an elementary school. Twenty years later, President Carter had to declare Love Canal a federal health emergency. In October 1948, the emissions from U.S. Steel's Zinc Works and its American Steel and Wire plant in Donora, PA, mixed with fog and were trapped for five days by an inversion layer. The pollutants, which included carbon monoxide, sulfur dioxide, and hydrogen fluoride, killed 20 people and made thousands sick. In 1952, London's reliance on coal for heat and electricity, combined with windless conditions and temperature inversion, caused the Great Smog that left thousands dead or sick. During the same time, Los Angeles started to suffer from a different kind of smog. In the LA Basin, the exhaust from millions of vehicles gets routinely trapped by LA's geography and weather patterns, generating widespread respiratory illness and some of the earliest environmental activism and protest. Throughout the 1950s and 1960s, several rivers in the United States were so polluted that they caught on fire. The most infamous was the Cuyahoga River, which flows into Lake Erie in Cleveland, OH. In the 1950s, a mysterious disease of the central nervous system started to afflict people living in and around Minamata, Japan. Researchers finally discovered that the 'Minamata Disease' was caused by the bioaccumulation of mercury in seafood. The source turned out to be methylmercury in the wastewater of a chemical factory owned by the Chisso Corporation.

By the late 1960s, the negative environmental consequences of industrial production and consumption started to galvanize civic and governmental action. Industry was no longer exclusively seen as the generators of wealth and progress but also as polluters that killed and sickened people and nature.[5] In addition, corporations were increasingly seen as irresponsible and untrustworthy. Many environmental NGOs were founded during this period: 1967 Environmental Defense Fund, 1969 Friends of the Earth, 1970 Natural Resources Defense Council, and 1971 Greenpeace. The first Earth Day in the United States was on April 22, 1970. The modern environmental movement was born.

The growth of the environmental movement is mirrored by the growth in environmental regulation. In response to the Great Smog, the UK Parliament passed the Clean Air Act of 1956. The United States government was also compelled into action by persistent pollution problems. Congress passed the Air Pollution Control Act in 1955 and the Clean Air Act in 1963. Sweeping amendments to the U.S. Federal Water Pollution Control Act of 1948 created the Clean Water Act in 1972. In 1970, President Nixon created the U.S. Environmental Protection Agency (EPA) so that the growing body of federal environmental regulations could be written and enforced by one executive organization. Environmental law was born, and with it mandatory pollution control, implemented and enforced through so-called command and control regulation.[6]

For businesses, mandatory pollution control is about environmental compliance; it's costly, but it's the law. Economists and business scholars assume that cost increases as businesses reduce pollution, which creates a powerful disincentive to do anything beyond compliance. It also means that in the standard playbook of environmental economics, there is an optimal level of pollution control where the marginal cost of pollution control exceeds the marginal cost of environmental damage. Reducing pollution beyond this point would cost more than the monetary value of the environmental damage it would avoid. This means that there is an 'optimal' level of pollution, a notion which is unsavory for many environmentalists. At the same time, the costliness of mandatory pollution control creates incentives for businesses to fight environmental regulation through lobbying, to avoid it by moving their production facilities to states or countries with less environmental regulation, or simply to shirk the regulation and hope to not get caught. In fact, economists would see shirking as perfectly rational behavior if the probability-weighted cost of getting caught is less than the savings of non-compliance. In such a world, business managers and environmentalists are clearly pitted against each other in a zero-sum game. One side's gain is the other one's loss. Environmentalism is a threat to companies' profits or even viability. Companies are unrelenting and unrepentant polluters. Environmental accidents and disasters continued to happen. The following names will sound sadly familiar to many readers: 1976 Seveso, 1978 Amoco Cadiz, 1979 Three Mile Island, 1984 Bhopal, 1986 Chernobyl, 1989 Exxon Valdez. These confirmed environmentalists' belief that progress could only be made through anti-corporate action, tough regulation, and strict enforcement.

In 1975, the mantra that environmental protection is costly and that more protection costs more received its single biggest blow in the form of 3M's Pollution Prevention Pays (3P) program. 3M started as Minnesota Mining and Manufacturing Company and takes pride in its spirit of innovation and collaboration. It is best known for the invention of masking tape, originally used in auto body paint shops, and countless other adhesive products, such as Scotch Tape and Post-it Notes. When 3M's staff vice president Dr. Joseph Ling started the now-famous 3P program, it was revolutionizing how everyone thought about pollution. In 3M's own words: "The 3P program is predicated on the belief that pollution prevention is more environmentally effective, technically sound and economical than conventional pollution control equipment."[7] The first radical statement in 3M's 3P message is that it is better to prevent pollution in the first place rather than attempting to control it after it has been generated. The second, even more radical statement, is that preventing rather than controlling pollution can actually save rather than cost money. This statement was nothing less than the birth of the win-win, or double dividend, paradigm in corporate environmental sustainability. 3M's 2016 Sustainability Report proudly points out that in its forty years of existence the 3P program prevented over 2.1 million tons of pollutants and saved nearly 2 billion dollars.[8] The cost savings generated by the 3P program suggest that the relationship between business and the environment does not have to be a zero-sum game. A final feature of the 3P program worth pointing out is that it is based on voluntary employee engagement in order to identify pollution prevention opportunities. Actively encouraging employees to think about and look for solutions to their companies' environmental issues is also a radical departure from business as usual.

Pollution prevention seemed to offer a viable alternative to costly pollution control and the constant fighting between companies, regulators, and environmentalists. Legislators and regulators in Europe and the United States soon embraced pollution prevention and made it an integral part of their national environmental policies. In 1990, the U.S. Congress even passed the Pollution Prevention Act, which states that "pollution should be prevented or reduced at the source whenever feasible."[9] It also emphasizes that, in contrast to costly pollution control, such source reduction offers substantial monetary savings. The win-win aspect of pollution prevention was very appealing to companies, many of which started their own programs. Examples are Dow Chemical's Waste Reduction Always Pays (WRAP) program and Chevron's Save Money and Reduce Toxics (SMART) program.

Leaded gasoline is not the only major environmental drama that was conceived in the lab of the General Motors Research Corporation. Another one is the synthesis of chlorofluorocarbons (CFCs). However, the story of CFCs developed differently than the story of leaded gasoline, which is worth exploring in some depth. In the late 1920s, Kettering and Midgely discovered that dichlorodifluoromethane (CFC-12), which they called Freon, is an excellent refrigerant.[10] Unlike the refrigerants that were being used in refrigerators and air conditioners at the time, it is also neither toxic nor flammable. GM and DuPont formed a joint venture to patent, mass produce, and market Freon. Additional CFCs were developed, patented, and marketed under the Freon brand name, the most important of which were CFC-11 and CFC-113. CFC-11 was mainly used as a blowing agent for foams. CFC-113's main use was as solvent to clean electronic components like printed circuit boards. CFC-11 and CFC-12 were also used as aerosol propellants. The large growth in refrigeration, air conditioning, spray cans, and electronics made Freon products a huge commercial success. In the 1970s, DuPont was still by far the largest and the only global CFC producer, even though its patents had run out.

A seminal publication by UC Irvine chemists Rowland and Molina in the science journal *Nature* in 1974 was therefore very bad news for DuPont. It suggested that CFCs, which are extremely stable molecules, are likely to migrate slowly to the stratosphere and act there as catalysts to convert ozone (O_3) to oxygen (O_2).[11] Stratospheric ozone is very important since it absorbs large amounts of ultraviolet (UV) radiation from the sun and thus protects humans, animals, and plants from excessive UV damage. Measurements in 1971 by British scientist James Lovelock had already shown that all CFC ever produced was still in the atmosphere.[12] A widespread depletion of the stratospheric ozone layer would be another major human-made environmental disaster on a global scale, just like worldwide lead pollution.

DuPont's initial response was twofold. On the one hand, it took out full-page newspaper ads to announce that it would stop production of CFCs if there was irrefutable evidence that showed that CFCs indeed caused a significant health threat. On the other hand, DuPont emphasized that the science was not solid enough to warrant the discontinuation of such useful compounds. This is a textbook application of the Kehoe Paradigm and the accompanying questioning of the science. However, it turned out that the days of CFC in spray cans were numbered anyway. Worried by press coverage of Rowland and Molina's discovery, American consumers started to switch to non-aerosol packaging for many products, such as deodorants. In 1975, consumer products company Johnson Wax (now SC Johnson) announced that it would phase out CFCs as aerosol propellants. Then-CEO Samuel Johnson published "An open letter to consumers about aerosols" in the *New York Times* explaining that he made that decision despite scientific uncertainty, essentially applying the precautionary principle. Other companies followed suit. In 1978, the U.S. EPA banned the use of CFCs in non-essential aerosols and stated that it is considering regulation for other CFC uses.

The resulting loss of the U.S. aerosol market was a wake-up call for DuPont, who again responded in two ways. Together with the other U.S. CFC manufacturers, it increased its efforts to avoid additional CFC regulation. Yet, at the same time, DuPont invested significant money and resources into looking for CFC substitutes, especially ones that could be patented. In the 1980s, evidence that CFCs were indeed thinning the ozone layer was hardening year by year. The international community was ready to move and, in 1987, agreed upon a plan to phase out production and use of CFCs in the famous Montreal Protocol on Substances that Deplete the Ozone Layer. In early 1988, DuPont was still arguing that "at the moment, scientific evidence does not point to the need for dramatic CFC emission reductions."[13] Then, ten days after the U.S. Senate ratified the Montreal Protocol 83–0, CEO Richard Heckert announced that DuPont would get out of the CFC business entirely. In 1991, DuPont would even suggest accelerating the planned phase-outs. It was also ready to roll out the CFC substitutes it had developed.

A publication that would forever change the way business scholars and students look at environmental issues came out in 1991. The one-page essay published in *Scientific American* was written by no one less than Michael Porter, the head of Harvard Business School's Competition and Strategy Group.[14] His statement that "the conflict between environmental protection and economic competitiveness is a false dichotomy" is now known as the Porter Hypothesis. Porter postulates that strict environmental regulation may generate rather than hamper competitive advantage. This was an endorsement and even an extension of the win-win paradigm. To appreciate just how momentous this was, consider that Porter is one of the gurus of business strategy, strategy is the most admired of all business school departments, and Harvard is the most admired of all business schools. In his essay, Porter mentions two companies by name: 3M and its 3P program and DuPont and its (eventual) support of a CFC phase-out. In a later and longer article in Harvard Business Review (HBR) with Claas van der Linde, Porter greatly expands the list of case studies and the theoretical underpinning of the win-win paradigm.[15] The HBR article promotes the view of 'pollution as resource inefficiency', which implies that pollution prevention, and to some extent even smart forms of pollution abatement, frequently combine environmental impact reduction with cost savings. While 3M is still the poster child of pollution prevention, the article abounds with additional examples. It also suggests that businesses with a proactive stance towards environmental regulation have a 'first mover advantage' which frequently translates into competitive advantage, as exemplified by DuPont's dominance of the market for CFC substitutes. The Porter Hypothesis thus argues that two mechanisms power the win-win paradigm: Improved resource productivity avoids pollution and saves cost, while good environmental regulation creates outside pressure on businesses which spurs innovation and thus competitive advantage. 'Good regulation', according to the HBR article, mandates pollution outcomes rather than pollution control technologies and uses market incentives instead of command and control.

The Earth Summit preparations were in full swing when Porter first published his hypothesis. That a Harvard Business School professor thought that protecting the environment can be reconciled with the goals of business was a welcome message after decades of stand-offs. Porter was not the only advocate of win-win at the time. Many business scholars and other academics shared his optimism, and double-dividends literature started to accumulate. Business leaders such as Stephan Schmidheiny, heir to fiber cement company Eternit, legislators such as Al Gore, future Vice President of the United States, and environmental NGOs such as Greenpeace Germany, all came to believe that business could, and should, be leaders in the pursuit of environmental sustainability. This new belief that it 'pays to be green' sounded almost too good to be true, and, in fact, fairly soon some started to claim that is was.

A good example is a 1994 HBR article from McKinsey consultants Noah Walley and Bradley Whitehead, who argue that for companies "win-win opportunities become insignificant in the face of the enormous environmental expenditures that will never generate a positive financial return."[16] According to Wally and Whitehead, win-win situations do exist but by now the most rewarding ones have already been implemented. This is also known as the 'low-hanging fruit' argument of the win-win debate. Yes, there are some, so the argument goes, but most of them have already been picked or will be picked shortly. Just like Porter, Wally and Whitehead backed up their claims with a series of case studies, in their case from the chemical, paper, and oil and gas industries. What ensued for the remainder of the 1990s was a heated debate about whether, in general, it pays or costs for companies to be green. The debate left a voluminous legacy in terms of reports, white papers, articles, and books.

Towards the end of the second millennium the debate settled, maybe unsurprisingly, on 'it depends'. Probably no other literature describes and represents this fairly common-sense viewpoint better than the publications of Forest Reinhardt, another professor at Harvard Business School. He points out that no other business issues are expected to have such categorical answers. Reinhardt also advises business scholars and managers to treat environmental problems like any other business problems, since companies aren't in the business to solve the world's environmental problems and shareholders want to see a return on their investments. Finally, he divides the instances in which it does potentially pay to be green into five different categories.[17] While these publications are twenty years old now, they still very much represent the state of the art of (business) scholarly thinking on business and the environment. What has not been settled yet, and is unlikely to be settled anytime soon, is the question whether win-win opportunities are widespread and significant or not.

Asking whether it pays to be green is just one way to investigate the win-win, or double dividend, paradigm. Sometimes this is also framed as the question of whether tightening environmental regulation will be costly to companies or not. Voluntary environmental activities of companies, i.e. environmental activities that go beyond mere compliance with environmental regulation, is frequently just called 'beyond compliance'. A third way to investigate the relationship between business and the environment is to ask whether companies should engage in beyond compliance behavior. Supporters of widespread win-win opportunities suggest that going beyond compliance is reconcilable with the profit-maximizing behavior typically assumed of firms. The opposing view argues that most beyond compliance behavior would be at odds with maximizing shareholder value. As a result, some argue that companies should exclusively focus on creating shareholder value while complying with all regulation.

Much of the post-Rio business and the environment literature, like Porter, Wally and Whitehead, and Reinhardt, has been criticized for its reliance on case studies. There is a risk that, even unknowingly, case studies are cherry-picked or presented in a skewed or incomplete way to support the arguments. One of the case studies in Porter and van der Linde's aforementioned HBR article is the East German company Foron, which used to be the largest producer of refrigerators in the Eastern Bloc but suffered badly after the German reunification. Once the Montreal Protocol was signed,

HFC-134a became the refrigerant of choice for many industries. It contains no chlorine but has 1,430 times the global warming potential of CO_2.[18] As the HBR article points out, Greenpeace Germany teamed up with Foron to produce and market the world's first mass-produced fridge, using a propane/isobutene mix as refrigerant instead of HFC-134a. It reads as a great example of a company teaming up with an environmental NGO to create a win-win scenario.

What the article doesn't say is that Foron went bankrupt once the major West German producers also started to offer propane/isobutene-based fridges, since Greenpeace didn't allow Foron to patent the technology.[19] Hydrocarbon-based refrigerants still have a difficult time penetrating the global market since the producers of CFC replacements work hard to portray it as dangerous. It took the U.S. EPA until March 2015 to finally allow the use of hydrocarbon-based refrigerants in the United States.

Reinhardt's assertion that one should not expect a categorical answer to the question "does it pay to be green?" has not stopped a significant number of business scholars from studying the relationship between environmental and economic performance of firms in order to look for just such a categorical relationship. These analyses usually examine whether and how environmental and economic performance measures of companies are correlated. This laudable attempt to use systematic empirical instead of anecdotal evidence faces several challenges and has not been able to generate conclusive results. Many would argue that the latter is unsurprising since a categorical relationship between green and profitable does not exist and thus can't be found. One of the research challenges, if one were to look anyway, is the selection of meaningful economic and, in particular, environmental performance measures. Business scholars are particularly cavalier when it comes to choosing indicators for corporate environmental performance and seem to readily equate environmental reputation or activity with actual environmental performance. The entire next chapter will thus explore the question of how to measure environmental performance. Another challenge is to identify the meaning of a positive correlation between an economic and an environmental indicator. Can you infer causality from the correlation? If so, which one is the cause, which one the effect? Does each one affect the other, creating a circular relationship called endogeneity and biasing the regression results? Or maybe both are effected by an unobserved external cause? Is something like a short-term dip in stock value after some corporate environmental event, like an accident or a lawsuit, even a meaningful signal?

It feels like the business and the environment discourse is at an impasse at the moment. The win-win rhetoric has gone stale, but there appears to be no alternative in sight, since no one dares to question the imperative of maximizing profits or shareholder value. Corporate sustainability scholars thus still feel obliged to look for those double dividends, but the 1990s enthusiasm is clearly gone. The win-win paradigm still dominates the corporate sustainability debate, but its promise rings increasingly hollow. Today, all win-win talk is overshadowed by reports of progressive environmental deterioration and increasingly sounds like whistling in the dark.

Notes

1   Donald J. Hughes and Jack V. Thirgood, "Deforestation, Erosion, and Forest Management in Ancient Greece and Rome," *Journal of Forest History* 26, no. 2 (1982): pp. 60–75, accessed July 21, 2020, www.jstor.org/stable/4004530. As told by classical writers of the time, deforestation in Ancient Rome was "widespread and severe" and assisted in leading to the "political and economic demise of the ancient world."

2   History.com Editors, "Ford Motor Company Unveils the Model T," *A&E Television Networks*, last modified November 13, 2009, accessed July 21, 2020, www.history.com/this-day-in-history/ford-motor-company-unveils-the-model-t.

3   Roland Geyer, "The Industrial Ecology of the Automobile," in *Taking Stock of Industrial Ecology*, Roland Clift and Angela Druckman (Eds.) (Berlin, Germany: Springer, 2016), pp. 331–341, https://link.springer.com/chapter/10.1007/978-3-319-20571-7_18; Kat Eschner, "Leaded Gas Was a Known Poison the Day It Was Invented," *Smithsonian Magazine*, last modified December 9, 2016, accessed July 21, 2020, www.smithsonianmag.com/smart-news/leaded-gas-poison-invented-180961368/.

4   Jerome O. Nriagu, "Clair Patterson and Robert Kehoe's Paradigm of 'Show Me the Data' on Environmental Lead Poisoning," *Environmental Research* 78, no. 2 (1998): pp. 71–78, accessed July 21, 2020, www.sciencedirect.com/science/article/abs/pii/S0013935197938081.

5   E.g. *Silent Spring* by Rachel Carson on the effects of pesticides on both human and environmental welfare (1962), and the 1971 children's book *The Lorax* by Dr. Seuss.

6   Command and control regulation works by 1) setting specific emission standards and/or mandating specific pollution control technologies and 2) enforcing compliance through monitoring programs and penalties for non-compliance.

7   Michele Ochsner, Caron Chess, and Michael Greenberg, "Pollution Prevention at the 3M Corporation: Case Study Insights into Organizational Incentives, Resources, and Strategies," *Waste Management* 15, no. 8 (1995): pp. 663–672, accessed July 21, 2020, www.sciencedirect.com/science/article/pii/0956053X96000475.

8   "3M 2016 Sustainability Report," *3M Company*, accessed July 21, 2020, https://multimedia.3m.com/mws/media/1214315O/2016-3m-sustainability-report.pdf.

9   Pollution Prevention Act of 1990 § 42 U.S.C § 13101(b) (1990).

10 Kat Eschner, "One Man Invented Two of the Deadliest Substances of the 20th Century," *Smithsonian Magazine*, last modified May 18, 2017, accessed July 21, 2020, www.smithsonianmag.com/smart-news/one-man-two-deadly-substances-20th-century-180963269/.

11 Mario J. Molina and F. S. Rowland, "Stratospheric Sink for Chlorofluoromethanes: Chlorine Atom-Catalysed Destruction of Ozone," *Nature* 249, no. 5460 (June 1974): pp. 810–812, accessed July 21, 2020, www.nature.com/articles/249810a0.

12 James E. Lovelock, "Atmospheric Fluorine Compounds as Indicators of Air Movements," *Nature* 230, no. 5293 (1971): p. 379, accessed January 13, 2021, www.nature.com/articles/230379a0.

13 "Du Pont Will Stop Making Ozone Killers," *Los Angeles Times*, last modified March 25, 1988, accessed January 13, 2021, www.latimes.com/archives/la-xpm-1988-03-25-mn-294-story.html.

14 Michael E. Porter, "America's Green Strategy," *Scientific American* 264, no. 4 (April 1991), accessed January 13, 2021, www.scientificamerican.com/article/essay-1991-04/.

15 Michael E. Porter and Claas van der Linde, "Green and Competitive: Ending the Stalemate," *Harvard Business Review* 73, no. 5 (September–October 1995): pp. 120–134, accessed January 13, 2021, https://hbr.org/1995/09/green-and-competitive-ending-the-stalemate.

16 Noah Walley and Bradley Whitehead, "It's Not Easy Being Green," *Harvard Business Review* 72, no. 3 (May-June 1994): pp. 46–52, accessed January 13, 2021, https://hbr.org/1994/05/its-not-easy-being-green.

17 Forest L. Reinhardt, "Bringing the Environment Down to Earth," *Harvard Business Review* 77, no. 4 (July-August 1999): pp. 149–149, accessed January 13, 2021, https://hbr.org/1999/07/bringing-the-environment-down-to-earth. The five categories Reinhardt mentions are 1) Differentiating Products, 2) Managing Your Competitors, 3) Saving Costs, 4) Managing Environmental Risk, and 5) Redefining Markets.

18 "Refrigerant Transition & Environmental Impacts," *U.S. Environmental Protection Agency*, accessed July 21, 2020, www.epa.gov/mvac/refrigerant-transition-environmental-impacts.

19 Christoph Gunkel, "Öko-Coup aus Ostdeutschland," *Spiegel*, last modified March 13, 2013, accessed January 13, 2021, www.spiegel.de/geschichte/oeko-revolution-aus-ostdeutschland-wie-foron-den-ersten-fckw-freien-kuehlschrank-der-welt-erfand-a-951064.html.

3

IT'S NOT EASY BEING GREEN WHEN YOU'RE COLOR BLIND

Early in 2011, I received a phone call from the CEO of a company that makes franchise products for the big Hollywood film studios; think plastic replicas or plush versions of Minions, superheroes, princesses, and Stormtroopers. He told me that Dr. Seuss' The Lorax was being made into a movie by Universal Studios and that he was in negotiations with the Dr. Seuss brand owners about the franchise toys for the film. A great opportunity but not without challenges, the CEO told me. "You see, the theme of The Lorax is highly environmental and therefore, to protect the brand image, all of the products must be green." He asked me if I knew the story. In 2011, my children were four and seven, and I replied that I knew The Lorax and many other Dr. Seuss books more or less by heart. Oh, the places you'll go! Do you like green eggs and ham? Just in case you're not familiar with the iconic Lorax, first published in 1971: It tells the story of a nifty entrepreneur, called Once-ler, who discovers a beautiful valley covered in Truffula trees and starts clear-cutting it in order to make Thneeds out of their soft, colorful foliage. Thneeds, which look a bit like adult onesies, are as irresistible as

DOI:10.4324/9781003163060-03

they are unnecessary, and soon the entire valley is deforested and polluted by the Thneed factory, thanks to runaway Thneed demand.

So, the challenge was to come up with Lorax-themed toys and collectables that were 'green', and I couldn't help feeling that there was a deep, intrinsically unresolvable contradiction in the entire enterprise. Green compared to what? One obvious proposal was recycled plastic. This immediately raised concerns about contaminants in the recycled plastic making the toys unsafe for small children, who have a tendency to suck and chew on everything. Making them out of recycled plastics was certainly greener than making them out of lead, but would it be greener than making them out of wood? Also, could it be argued that making them smaller made them greener since they would use less material? The one thing I could say with certainty is that it really made me think hard about what constitutes a 'green' product. After about a month I received an email from the CEO informing me that "sadly the Seuss team rejected the idea of products for the Lorax movie." This outcome confirmed my looming suspicion that there was no unambiguous definition of a green movie franchise toy. There is no franchise toy made of recycled plastic or driftwood or made however small that could possibly be greener than no toy at all.

When business scholars and businesses began to embrace the win-win/double dividend paradigm and rhetoric, they also had to start thinking about what 'being green' actually meant. This turned out to be much harder than they anticipated or even realized.

It's pretty simple to define 'profitable', the predominant concern of the business community. It essentially boils down to some version of 'revenues are larger than costs', so maybe business scholars expected 'green' to be similarly straightforward. It is no exaggeration to say that there was, and still is, enormous naivety at business schools and businesses alike when it comes to the notion of 'green'. I sat through entire presentations at top-rated business schools about the market diffusion of green innovations without the speaker ever bothering to explain what, exactly, that green innovation was supposed to be. Remarkably, I seemed to be the only one troubled by this. The talk was entirely focused on some twist of Frank Bass' famous product diffusion model (first introduced in 1969), and the greenness of the innovation was just something that allowed for customer differentiation, since they would have different preferences for said 'greenness'.[1]

While my colleagues in the technology management department of a famous business school conducted cutting-edge operations research to integrate product remanufacturing, component reuse, and material recycling into sophisticated inventory and scheduling models, I was stuck wondering whether remanufacturing, reuse, and recycling were 'green' to begin with. Indeed, the fact that no one at a business school was ever able to give me a meaningful definition of what a green product or business practice is, is the reason I decided to get my PhD at Professor Clift's Centre for Environmental Strategy rather than a business school. The win-win debate and literature themselves, which arguably created the need to define 'green' in the first place, are mostly focused on the economic piece of the puzzle and surprisingly unconcerned with the definition of environmental performance. A substantial amount of qualitative and quantitative research on the win-win hypothesis has come out of business schools. As mentioned earlier, much of the quantitative research investigates whether economic and environmental performance of companies are positively correlated; in other words, whether businesses with better economic performance tend to have better environmental performance and/or vice versa. The standard tool to study this is called regression analysis. However, even the most sophisticated and rigorous regression analysis of corporate environmental and economic performance data is useless if the environmental performance measure is flawed.

One standard approach to greenness used by the business community and business literature alike is the concept of green or environmental product attributes. Especially in marketing, practitioners and researchers are used to characterizing products in terms of product attributes, which, in turn, determine production cost on the one hand and customer preference on the other. This is the framework used by Forest Reinhardt and others to discuss environmental product differentiation.[2] It is frequently assumed that increasing the greenness of a product will increase its cost and thus require customers to pay a price premium for the environmental attributes of the product. Examples used by Reinhardt are the use of polyester made from recycled PET (polyethylene terephthalate) plastic or the use of organic cotton to make clothing. Recycled PET and organic cotton, he says, make apparel greener but also more expensive, so the customer must be willing to pay more for the increase in environmental product performance. That using recycled PET or organic cotton makes products greener is not shown but simply assumed. In another case study, Reinhardt introduces Monsanto's herbicide Roundup as a green product since it supposedly eliminates or at least reduces the need for tillage.[3] Later in the case study, he does admit that there is considerable controversy surrounding the environmental benefits of Roundup and Roundup Ready crops, i.e. crops genetically engineered to withstand the herbicide. Since then, glyphosate, the active ingredient in Roundup, has been found in myriads of food items and been listed by the World Health Organization as "probably carcinogenic in humans."[4]

With such a cavalier approach to environmental product performance, many things can be deemed green without any real analysis. Products with recycled material become green because recycling is good for the environment. Clothes made from natural fibers are green because they are made from renewable resources. So are biofuels and bioplastics. Or maybe biofuels are green because growing the fuel crop sequesters carbon dioxide, and bioplastics are green because they biodegrade. Electric vehicles are green because they have no tailpipe emissions. And a hybrid car is green because, well, it's a hybrid, right? One California company now sells sparkling water shipped from New Zealand and bottled in single-use aluminum bottles and considers it "truly sustainable water," pointing out that their aluminum bottle is "resealable" and "80% lighter than a glass bottle of the same size."[5] I once even heard an architect describe the Gateshead Millennium Bridge over the River Tyne in Newcastle, UK, as sustainable, because "it connects people."

The notion of green becomes even more elusive when companies don't sell conventional products but offer services instead. This is unfortunate since selling services instead of products, sometimes called servicizing, has long been seen as an important way to reduce corporate environmental impact. For many years, servicizing was more popular as a corporate sustainability concept than an actual business practice, but the advent of the sharing economy has given this longstanding and long-loved idea renewed relevance. Providers such as Uber, Airbnb, and Zipcar and their users more or less automatically assume that sharing services generate environmental benefits, a notion that has also been readily accepted by most corporate sustainability professionals and scholars. In fact, during my time at the aforementioned business school, car sharing was one of those 'green innovations' that my colleagues loved to talk about. But is it really green?

In this paragraph, I will lay out the argument that car sharing has no intrinsic environmental benefits relative to conventional car ownership. I invite you to deconstruct and challenge the argument after you've read it. In Chapter 6, we will revisit and solve the car-sharing conundrum. The argument goes like this: Let's assume that car owners drive, on average, 12,500 km per year, and that on average cars last and are driven for 200,000 km. Seeing that $200,000 / 12,500 = 16$, this means that under average usage an average car lasts 16 years. It follows that in 16 years 100 car owners would drive 20 million kilometers and go through 100 cars. Now, let's assume that, instead of owning cars, those 100 people share 20 cars between them, i.e. there is one car per five people. This means that, on average, each shared car is driven $5 \times 12,500$ km $= 62,500$ km per year and therefore needs to be retired after $200,000 / 62,500 = 3.2$ years. Replacing 20 cars every 3.2 years means that, after $5 \times 3.2 = 16$ years, the 100 car sharers have used up $5 \times 20 = 100$ cars – the exact same amount that the 100 car owners went through. And the car sharers also drove the same amount of cumulative distance, $100 \times 12,500 \times 16 = 20$ million kilometers. I thus conclude that car sharing has the same environmental impact as car ownership. Do you agree? Or is this argument flawed or incomplete? We will answer the second question in Chapter 6 where we revisit the car-sharing case study.

Now, the environmental sustainability of a company may manifest itself not only through the greenness of its products and services, however defined, but also through its business practices and processes. Complementary to the study of green products and services, the business school literature therefore also studies green business practices and behaviors and their relationship to economic performance. The traditional approach to green businesses is not too dissimilar to the concept of green product attributes. Practices are grouped into categories or issues, such as 'pollution prevention', 'recycling', 'clean energy', 'management systems', 'hazardous waste', 'regulatory problems', and 'substantial emissions'.[6] Companies are then rated or scored in each of these categories, and the scores are aggregated, possibly after being weighted. The higher the total score, the greener the company. Such rating or scoring attempts are laudable but also clearly problematic. There is a high risk of subjectivity, large reliance on anecdotal evidence and qualitative information, and abundant use of proxies, which may or may not be good indicators for actual environmental performance. There is, for example, an ongoing debate whether the use of environmental management systems, such as ISO 14000, leads to significant environmental outcomes. The use of an aggregate score based on a diverse set of issues also makes one wonder how robust green rankings of companies are, especially across sectors or industries, and how meaningful.

Another issue that complicates the environmental assessment of business practices is the fact that most, if not all, companies are part of a larger supply or value chain and thus intrinsically linked with upstream suppliers and downstream customers. This raises the question to what extent the upstream and downstream production and consumption processes should be counted towards a company's environmental performance. An excellent demonstration of this issue is Dell's experience when it announced in August 2008 that it had become 'carbon neutral'. Later that year, the Wall Street Journal pointed out that the greenhouse gas emissions that Dell counted towards its carbon footprint were limited to the fuels and electricity used in its buildings, the company-owned cars, and during its employees' air travel.[7] This amounted to 0.49 million metric tons (Mt) of carbon dioxide equivalent (CO_2e) in the fiscal year 2007/2008. Dell also estimated that, in the same year, the emissions associated with making and using its computers and servers were around 5 Mt each.[8] In other words, by limiting the definition of its carbon footprint to its corporate boundaries, Dell excluded over 95% of the annual emissions associated with making and using its products. Unsurprisingly, Dell received a fair amount of ridicule for its claim of carbon neutrality.

An interesting side note is that the vast majority of the 0.49 Mt CO_2e were not eliminated but offset through purchased renewable energy credits and carbon credits from investments in forest preservation projects. The Dell experience exemplifies the ongoing discussions about the extent to which emission offsets and credits are equivalent to actual emission reductions and the extent to which companies should take responsibility of their upstream and downstream emissions. How do you compare companies that make the same type of products but have different levels of vertical integration? In other words, how do you compare a company that makes its own components and assembles them into their products to one that only designs the products and has others make the components and assemble them? It is very problematic, to say the least, if a company would be able to increase its environmental performance simply by outsourcing processes with high environmental impact.

There is a significant number of people who would argue that some, if not all, of these issues can be addressed by the use of life cycle assessment (LCA) or at least life cycle thinking. The conceptual and formal development of life cycle assessment was most certainly a milestone in corporate environmental management, and LCA is now one of the most powerful tools for measuring corporate environmental impact.[9] I will therefore spend the remainder of this chapter explaining the concept, its power, and its limitations.

LCA has its name from the vital insight that products, and thus the services derived from them, can cause environmental impacts at all stages of their life cycles. A product life cycle consists of material and energy resource extraction, material and component production, product assembly, distribution, use, and end of life. To truly understand a product's or service's impact on the natural environment, all stages of its life cycle need to be examined. In order to combine or compare the various impacts along a product's life cycle, an ideally quantitative framework is needed, the development of which started together with the dawn of the modern environmental movement in the late 1960s and early 1970s.

One of the earliest examples was a comparison of beverage containers in 1969, conceived and funded by Coca-Cola and conducted by the Midwest Research Institute, a contract research organization based in Kansas City, MO. According to two of the analysts involved in the study, its goal was "to quantify the energy, material, and environmental consequences of a package from the extraction of raw materials to disposal."[10] The studied containers were glass bottles, aluminum cans, and plastic bottles, which Coca-Cola wasn't using yet. Back then, these studies were called resource and environmental profile analyses (REPAs). The time was clearly ripe for life cycle thinking since life cycle assessment methods were developed at the same time at different organizations and in different countries. As the number of life cycle studies increased over the years, their limitations and shortcomings also become more apparent.

One such shortcoming was the lack of agreed-upon methods. One could frequently guess the results of an environmental life cycle comparison between products by determining which product the commissioner of the study had a stake in. If there was another LCA, commissioned by an organization with a stake in the other product, it was likely to come to the opposite conclusion. This was clearly threatening the credibility of LCA as an objective tool for environmental decision making – be it by policy makers, companies, or consumers.

A famous example was the diaper controversy of 1990/91. In the 1960s, Proctor & Gamble (P&G) launched Pampers disposable diapers, essentially creating a new product category. By converting cloth-diaper users to disposable diapers, P&G experienced incredible growth in sales and revenues. By the mid-1970s, P&G sold Pampers in 75 countries and had 75% market share in the United States. But when studies showed in the late 1980s that disposable diapers alone made up 1–3% of household waste, they came under fire from environmental and consumer advocacy groups, who started to brandish single-use diapers as a symbol of the 'throw-away society'.[11] P&G responded by charging consultancy Arthur D. Little with a comparative LCA, which concluded that, while reusable diapers generated much less solid waste, they used over three times more energy and over six times more water than disposable ones.[12] The National Association of Diaper Services and environmental groups countered with their own LCAs, claiming that disposable diapers, in fact, used more energy and water than reusable ones.[13] So, rather than settling the debate, these LCAs confused the public and thus seemed a bit useless.

To address this issue, the Society of Environmental Toxicology and Chemistry (SETAC) started a process of harmonizing LCA theory and practice in the early 1990s. SETAC was founded in 1979 and was itself an outcome of the modern environmental movement and the environmental regulation it spawned. In 1993, it published its seminal *Guidelines for Life-Cycle Assessment: A 'Code of Practice'*. This was the birth of LCA as we know and use it today. Standardization efforts continued throughout the 1990s, now through the International Organization for Standardization (ISO), which led to ISO standards for LCA. A revision in 2006 gave us ISO 14040 and 14044, the current gold standards for LCA.[14]

Let's use the example of beverage containers to illustrate the power of LCA. The first important insight is that one cannot simply compare the packaging materials, aluminum, glass, and plastic directly with each other or compare three random containers made from these materials. To compare apples with apples, the compared containers need to provide the same amount of service, here containing and protecting a given amount of beverage. Since containers come in many different sizes, this is not a trivial task. Let's assume, for simplicity's sake, that containing 1 liter of beverage requires around 38 grams of aluminum cans, 40 grams of polyethylene terephthalate (PET) bottles, and 450 grams of glass bottles. That's roughly three cans and glass bottles and two PET bottles (the plastic that soda bottles are made of), assuming their sizes are 330 ml or 12 fl. oz. and 500ml or 20 fl. oz., respectively.

Next, all processes that are involved in the production, transportation, use, and disposal of these beverage containers need to be identified and quantified in terms of their environmental impact. This is the heart of LCA and where things can get complicated. For the moment, let's just assume that, with the help of the ISO standards, we were able to generate table 3.1.

Before the aluminum, plastic, and glass industry associations start sending me complaints about misrepresenting the environmental performance of their material: The table is just for illustrative purposes. While the GHG emission numbers in the table are certainly in the ballpark, they do come from a fairly simple analysis rather than a comprehensive LCA. Yet even such a simple analysis generates valuable insights, which withstand the scrutiny of more detailed assessments.

First, the common view that glass bottles are a bad environmental choice because of the transportation impacts caused by their high weight is incorrect. It is true that a container that has ten times the weight of an alternative is likely to have ten times the environmental impact from transportation. However, LCAs of beverage containers and other packaging consistently show that transportation contributes only a small fraction to the total life cycle impact. Instead, it is the production of the packaging material that typically generates the lion's share of the life cycle impact.

Second, assuming that the container with the smallest mass must also have the lowest impact is also wrong. Making primary aluminum from ore

Table 3.1 An example for life cycle GHG emissions (measured in grams of CO_2e) of three beverage containers (for illustration purposes only)

	Material production	Container forming	Container transportation	Disposal/ recycling	Total
Aluminum can (38g)	534	42	6	−332	250
PET bottle (40g)	96	37	7	−22	118
Glass bottle (450g)	435		63	−23	475

(called bauxite) is very GHG intensive, so, without recycling, aluminum cans would have the highest life cycle GHG emissions, despite being the lightest of the three containers.

However, collecting and recycling aluminum cans back into new cans has much lower GHG emissions than making primary aluminum cans. The resulting recycling credit brings the life cycle emissions below those of the glass bottle. However, with or without recycling, PET bottles are typically shown to have low life cycle GHG emissions compared to the alternatives.

In summary, LCA taught us that material production drives the environmental impacts of beverage containers, while transportation tends to be a small fraction of the total, unless it's done very inefficiently (think airfreight) and over very long distances. We also learned that the potential benefits from recycling depend on the material and are particularly large for aluminum. Not bad for a back-of-the-envelope analysis.

That is not to say that LCA is not without its challenges and controversies. Even the ISO standards were not able to resolve all outstanding issues and, in all fairness, were not expected to do so. The most notorious one, often simply called 'the allocation issue', comes from the fact that many production processes have more than one useful output. Some of the GHG emissions from container transportation, for example, come from the production of the diesel used by the trucks. Diesel comes from refineries that make many other fuels and also non-fuel products like lubricants and chemical feedstocks. Such joint production raises the question of how the GHG emissions from the refinery should be 'allocated' to all its outputs, since they are caused jointly and can't be traced to individual refinery products. This issue is not dissimilar to the accounting question of how to allocate overhead cost of a plant to individual products that are made in it, hence the name 'allocation issue'.

Another challenge is to determine which processes need to be included in the LCA and which ones can be excluded without distorting the results. This is known as system boundary selection in LCA. The issue at hand is that not everything involved in the product life cycle can be practically included, but nothing should be left out that has a significant contribution to the total life cycle impacts. This creates a bit of a Catch-22 since one needs to know the contribution of a particular process to determine whether it is significant, but the whole point of leaving it out is not having to assess it.

Capital equipment is a great example. PET bottles are formed by so-called stretch blow molding machines. The electricity used by the machine is what generates most of the GHG emissions of PET bottle forming shown in table 3.1. But should the production of the machine also be included? The GHG emissions of making the machine would have to be divided by its lifetime bottle output, which may be billions. So, even if producing such a machine has large impacts, the impact per bottle would be very small, which is why the production of capital equipment is frequently excluded from LCAs. However, someone had to include it first to determine that it can be excluded. Also, it turns out that this insight is not true for all types of capital equipment.

There is a considerable list of additional challenges that we needn't discuss here in detail. Standard LCAs lack spatial granularity or supply chain specificity. The most specific material production data, be it for steel, plastic, soy beans, or corn, are typically country averages. LCAs have many different environmental indicators. In addition to climate change impacts, an LCA may also estimate potential impacts from environmental concerns such as acidification, eutrophication, respiratory health, and toxicity. The beverage containers from our case study would thus be compared across a range of environmental impact categories with the possibility of inconclusive results. What if glass bottles have the highest climate change impact but the lowest toxicity impact? Such trade-offs across impact categories complicate the use of LCA for environmental decision making. It is tempting to combine all impact indicators into one environmental score, but this is always based on subjective value judgements and just hides these very real trade-offs.

Even assuming that these are all issues that can be resolved leaves two fundamental problems that I want to close this chapter with. The first is the use of benchmark products to determine greenness. LCA helps you conclude that a hybrid SUV is indeed greener than an equal-sized conventional SUV. But what if the customer chooses the hybrid SUV instead of a conventional compact car with higher fuel economy? The benchmark idea can be just as problematic for intermediate goods. An example would be a utility that chooses electricity from natural gas over renewable electricity and not over coal-based electricity as is typically assumed. Suddenly, the hybrid SUV and electricity from natural gas are not green anymore. You may contend that these examples demonstrate that the benchmark product needs to be chosen carefully, but the problem runs deeper than that. It can be argued that packaging made from recycled plastic is green compared to identical packaging from the virgin polymer. But a consumer may buy produce in recycled plastic clamshells instead of buying it without any packaging at all. The benchmark would now be no packaging at all, which means that no type of packaging could possibly be green. Imagine someone buying a refurbished cell phone (or any other refurbished electronic device) in addition to, rather than instead of, a new one, say as a backup device. Or picture someone buying the refurbished product because she cannot afford a new one. What about someone who buys a brand new, very energy-efficient gadget, not instead of a less energy-efficient gadget but instead of no gadget at all? Maybe the advertised greenness of the energy-efficient gadget even encouraged the consumer to purchase it instead of not buying anything. And remember the riddle of finding green franchise toys for the *Lorax* movie?

Finally, the elusive benchmark product points to the biggest issue of them all when it comes to defining green products through LCA. Just like the carbon intensity of GDP from Chapter 1, all LCA results are eco-efficiency measures, i.e. ratios of environmental impact over economic output. Our beverage container case study, for example, measured life cycle GHG emissions per liter of packaged beverage. The fact that business scholars and businesses themselves increasingly and fairly exclusively use eco-efficiency measures to determine greenness is so important and problematic that the entire next chapter is dedicated to it.

Notes

1 Frank Bass, "A New Product Growth Model for Consumer Durables," *Management Science* 15, no. 5 (1969): pp. 215–227, accessed January 13, 2021, www.jstor.org/stable/2628128.

2 Forest Reinhardt, "Environmental Product Differentiation: Implications for Corporate Strategy," *California Management Review* 40, no. 4 (1998): pp. 43–73, accessed January 13, 2021, https://doi.org/10.2307%2F41165964.

3 Forest Reinhardt, "Environmental Product Differentiation: Implications for Corporate Strategy," *California Management Review* 40, no. 4 (1998): pp. 43–73, accessed January 13, 2021, https://doi.org/10.2307%2F41165964.

4   "IARC Monograph on Glyphosate," *International Agency for Research on Cancer,* accessed July 21, 2020, www.iarc.fr/featured-news/media-centre-iarc-news-glyphosate/.

5   "Sustainability," *KOPU Water,* accessed January 3, 2021, https://kopuwater.com/sustainability/.

6   Magali Delmas and Vered Blass, "Measuring Corporate Environmental Performance: The Trade-Offs of Sustainability Ratings," *Business Strategy and the Environment* 19, no. 4 (2010): pp. 245–260, accessed January 13, 2021, www.researchgate.net/publication/229882659_Measuring _Corporate_ Environmental_Performance_The_Trade-Offs_of_Sustainability_Ratings.

7   Jeffrey Ball, "Green Goal of 'Carbon Neutrality' Hits Limit," *Wall Street Journal,* last modified December 30, 2008, accessed January 13, 2021, www.wsj.com/articles/SB123059880241541259.

8   Jeffrey Ball, "Green Goal of 'Carbon Neutrality' Hits Limit," *Wall Street Journal,* last modified December 30, 2008, accessed January 13, 2021, www.wsj.com/articles/SB123059880241541259.

9   Rita Schenck and Philip White (Eds.), *Environmental Life Cycle Assessment* (Bethesda, MD: American Center for Life Cycle Assessment, 2014).

10   Robert Hunt, William Franklin, and R. G. Hunt, "LCA – How It Came About," *The International Journal of Life Cycle Assessment* 1 (1996): pp. 4–7, accessed January 13, 2021, https://doi.org/10.1007/BF02978624.

11   "The Procter & Gamble Company: Disposable and Reusable Diapers – A Life-Cycle Analysis," *World Resources Institute,* (1994), accessed January 13, 2021, http://pdf.wri.org/bell/case_1-56973-167-5_full_version_english.pdf.

12   "Disposable Versus Reusable Diapers: Health, Environmental, and Economic Comparisons: Report to Procter and Gamble," *Arthur D. Little, Inc.,* (March 16, 1990), accessed January 13, 2021, https://p2infohouse.org/ref/31/30950.pdf.

13   Carl Lehrburger, Jocelyn Mullen, and C. V. Jones, "Diapers: Environmental Impacts and Lifecycle Analysis," *National Association of Diaper Services,* (January 1991), accessed January 13, 2021, https://p2infohouse.org/ref/30/29640.pdf.

14   Walter Klöpffer (Ed.), *Background and Future Prospects in Life Cycle Assessment* (Dordrecht, Holland: Springer, 2014).

4

THE PROBLEM WITH ECO-EFFICIENCY

James Watt was an incredible inventor, but he did not invent the steam engine. Instead, the first commercially successful steam engine was invented by Thomas Newcomen in 1712. It is called atmospheric (or simply Newcomen) engine and was used across Britain and the rest of Europe, mostly to pump water out of mines. It was the first practical device to convert heat/steam into mechanical work using a piston and cylinder design. In the Newcomen engine, the steam isn't used to push the piston out, as you might imagine. That's what's happening in a high-pressure steam engine, where the pressure is high enough to push the piston outwards. In Newcomen's engine, the pressure isn't high enough to do that. Instead, the power stroke happens when the piston is sucked inwards by the vacuum that is generated when some cold water is sprayed into the steam-filled cylinder and the steam condenses back to water as a result. Unfortunately, this is extremely inefficient. The cold water not only condenses the steam but also cools down the cylinder. So, most of the heat from the new steam

DOI:10.4324/9781003163060-04

entering the cylinder during the next stroke is used to reheat the cylinder walls rather than move the piston.

In 1765, James Watt realized that the energy loss in Newcomen's engine could be greatly reduced if the steam was condensed in a separate chamber called the external condenser. This way the cylinder could be kept at its hot operating temperature throughout, roughly doubling the energy efficiency of the Newcomen engine. Watt made many additional improvements to his steam engine and was thus a true efficiency pioneer. In other words, the industrial revolution didn't start with the invention of the steam engine but with a dramatic increase in its efficiency.

Exactly one hundred years after Watt's great breakthrough, in 1865, economist and logician William Stanley Jevons published his seminal book *The Coal Question; An Inquiry Concerning the Progress of the Nation, and the Probable Exhaustion of Our Coal Mines.* It touches on many modern-sounding themes, such as the role of (fossil) energy as factor of production, the implications of exponential growth, and the potential role of renewable energy. Most importantly for us, Jevons observed that the switch from Newcomen's to Watt's much more efficient steam engine design had greatly increased coal consumption in England. He famously says in the book: "It is wholly a confusion of ideas to suppose that the economical use of fuel is equivalent to a diminished consumption. The very contrary is the truth."[1] This early observation of energy efficiency gains increasing rather than decreasing energy consumption is now known as Jevons Paradox.

While coal production did peak in the UK in 1913, there was plenty more to be found elsewhere in the world, which also increasingly turned to crude oil and natural gas as fuels. Jevons' warnings were all but forgotten until the oil crises of the 1970s rekindled public interest in energy efficiency. Countries like the UK and the United States had become increasingly dependent on fossil fuel imports, and more efficient use of energy was seen as an important way to reduce energy consumption and thus reliance on fossil fuel imports. The standard assumption in energy policies and demand forecasts was, and still is, that an increase in energy efficiency translates one-to-one into energy use reductions. In other words, it is assumed that doubling the energy efficiency of a car fleet would cut its fuel consumption in half. Leonard Brookes in the UK and Daniel Khazzoom in the U.S. warned against such simplistic conjectures, essentially reviving and expanding upon Jevons' ideas.[2]

That increases in energy efficiency might, at least to some extent, stimulate energy use is now known as 'rebound effect'. The rebound literature distinguishes between three different types of rebound effect: Direct, indirect, and system- or economy-wide. The easiest to study empirically is the 'direct rebound effect'. Its basic premise is that an increase in the energy efficiency of a technology makes the use of that technology cheaper and will thus lead to an increased use of it. The most studied energy services are personal transportation (cars) and residential heating, cooling, and lighting. For economists studying direct rebound, increasing the efficiency of the technology is identical to a decrease in the cost of the energy input. Whether the price of gasoline goes down or the fuel efficiency of the car goes up, the result is that the owner can drive the same distance for less money. The question now is whether the owner uses some of the savings to drive more, thus creating direct rebound, and if yes, by how much. Knowing the price elasticity of the owner's driving demand would enable us to quantify the rebound effect, but price elasticities are notoriously difficult to estimate. Researchers therefore use all kinds of methods to estimate the size of direct rebound effects, with a wide range of results. According to reviews of direct rebound estimates, personal transportation shows a range of 20–65% and residential heating 30–60%, but lower and higher numbers can also be found in literature.[3]

By far the most efficient residential heating technology are heat pumps because they move existing heat rather than having to generate heat. Think of a refrigerator run backwards. Heat is absorbed from the outside and moved into the house. Using electricity to move heat can be up to four times as efficient as converting electricity into heat. One in four homes in Norway now use heat pumps.[4] Unfortunately, a 2013 study by the Norwegian statistics bureau found that these households use their heating cost savings to have warmer homes and that the "rebound effects are as great as the energy-savings potential of the heat pumps."[5]

Households that save money thanks to more efficient cars or heating may choose to spend their cost savings on other goods and services. This is called 'indirect rebound effect' and even harder to estimate than the direct rebound effect. What is certain is that households can only do two things with cost savings from increased energy efficiency: Save it or spend it. Low savings rates of households thus mean that indirect rebound will occur. The size of the energy footprints of the goods and services bought with the energy cost savings determines the size of the indirect rebound effect. Since life cycle studies show that virtually all goods and services have an energy footprint, indirect rebound will happen even if households do not use their energy cost savings to buy other forms of energy, say, use gasoline cost savings to purchase more natural gas and electricity for heating, cooling, or other energy services. In other words, spending the cost savings on food or furniture will still create indirect rebound due to the energy it took to make and transport these goods. Robust estimates of the indirect rebound effect are lacking, but some studies suggest that direct and indirect rebound combined could be anywhere between 30% and over 100%.[6] A rebound effect larger than 100% is called backfire and means that, just like in Jevons Paradox, the efficiency gain increases total energy consumption.

You might conclude that the safest way to avoid rebound is to put the energy cost savings from efficiency increases into your savings account. Unfortunately, that won't work either. Your savings are someone else's loans, frequently used to start or grow businesses and thus grow the economy. Economic activity, just like household spending, has an energy footprint (energy used per dollar GDP), so higher GDP means higher energy use, all other things being equal. This and other effects relating efficiency improvements to overall societal energy use are called 'economy-wide rebound'. It is the most comprehensive, and therefore most important, rebound effect but also the hardest to study.

As Brookes was inspired by Jevons, economist Harry Saunders was inspired by the work of Brookes and Khazzoom and, in 1992, formulated the Khazzoom-Brookes postulate. It says that "with fixed real energy price, energy efficiency gains will increase energy consumption above where it would be without these gains."[7] In other words, increases in efficiency cause economy-wide backfire. Saunders investigated his postulate using neoclassical growth theory, which tries to explain economic output (GDP) as a function of capital and labor input (called production factors) and a third variable that is supposed to capture technological progress. Saunders adds energy use as a production factor and shows that technical progress in the form of energy efficiency gains can lead to economic growth that will result in an increase in total energy use, i.e. cause economy-wide backfire. Needless to say, the Khazzoom-Brookes postulate is hotly disputed, and there is no consensus in sight. Some argue that efficiency gains are one of the main drivers of economic growth by increasing factor productivity. Others argue that energy use should not be a production factor at all since it is not a cause but a result of economic production. In fact, much of the criticism of the rebound effect focuses on the causality it implies between efficiency gains and energy use. Unfortunately, proving causality is much harder than just showing correlation.

In 1992, while Saunders was warning us against the unintended consequences of energy efficiency gains, efficiency was being promoted by others as the main tool to help industry and all its companies onto a sustainable course. A key figure behind this was Stephan Schmidheiny, who had inherited the asbestos-cement company Eternit in 1976. Asbestos is a naturally occurring mineral fiber that causes severe and fatal illnesses. The claim that combining it with cement would eliminate the health risks turned out to be incorrect. Schmidheiny's exit from Eternit in the late 1980s is controversial and even led to a prison sentence in 2012, which was overturned two years later. In 1990, he was appointed Principal Advisor for Business and Industry to the Secretary General of the 1992 Earth Summit and founded the Business Council for Sustainable Development (BCSD), which later added the word 'World' to become the WBCSD. In 1992, Schmidheiny and the BCSD published the influential book Changing Course, which popularized the notion of 'eco-efficiency' introduced in Chapter 1. In his own words, "the book shows how enterprises can combine environmental protection with economic growth."[8] Eco-efficiency is the key to this conundrum. As a quantitative measure, eco-efficiency is a summary term for pretty much any ratio between an environmental and an economic indicator and therefore denotes the amount of environmental impact per unit of economic output. There are many different types of environmental concerns, ranging from resource extraction, land and water use, to climate change, acidification, eutrophication, and human and ecological toxicity. Each concern tends to have several competing indicators, while economic output can also be quantified in many different ways. In Chapter 1, we used grams of CO_2 equivalent per dollar GDP to introduce eco-efficiency. In Chapter 3, we used grams of CO_2 equivalent per 1 liter of beverage container to explain life cycle assessment (LCA). Both quantify climate change impacts per unit of economic output. There are many, many more eco-efficiency indicators, and it is possible to forge entire careers with the development of new ones. As mentioned in Chapter 1, there are also many different names for the idea of investigating environmental impact per unit output or vice versa.

The promotion of eco-efficiency was part of a remarkable development that happened right at the time when the preparations for the Earth Summit where in full swing; suddenly, business was no longer inevitably the enemy of environmental protection and therefore no longer a clear and simple target for environmental regulation and activism. At least enlightened business wasn't. Environmental protection was now part of 'sustainable development', which also includes economic and social goals. And as it still says on Schmidheiny's personal website: "Business is good for sustainable development and sustainable development is good for business."[9] At the same time, Michael Porter formulated his famous hypothesis that environmental protection is, in fact, good for economic competitiveness, not bad as everyone had previously assumed.[10] All this was a remarkable one-eighty from 'us versus them' to 'win-win' opportunities or even 'win-win-win' if social goals were included. Integrating environmental protection with social equity and economic development or growth is rooted in the recognition that there are many linkages between the three. However, conflating the three issues also has the risk of obfuscating things.

The term sustainable development (SD) was popularized and defined by the World Commission on Environment and Development, also known as the Brundtland Commission, in their 1987 report called "Our Common Future."[11] The famous Brundtland definition of SD is so overused and

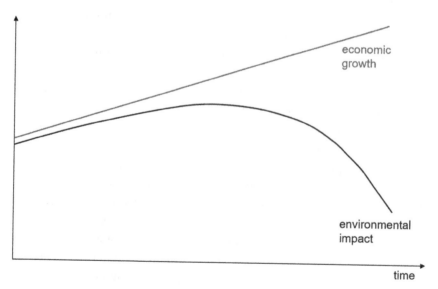

Figure 4.1 A typical illustration of decoupling[12]

toothless that I can't bring myself to quote it here. You can google it. Suffice it to say that it is about not wrecking the planet for future generations. The big SD conflation in the Brundtland report however went like this: Many parts of the world are still woefully poor; the social dimension of SD thus requires substantial and sustained economic growth. The environmental dimension of SD, on the other hand, requires that we arrest and revert environmental degradation. But how to reconcile the imperative of economic growth with the need for environmental sustainability? By becoming more eco-efficient. Eco-efficiency is the linchpin that holds the vision of growth plus sustainability together. Without eco-efficiency, the wheels come flying off the notion of sustainable growth.

The way eco-efficiency squares the circle of sustainable growth is by 'decoupling' environmental impact from economic growth; "doing more with less" as the WBCSD likes to say.[13] Decoupling is the ideological twin of eco-efficiency. An introduction to eco-efficiency is usually followed by an explanation of decoupling. The latter is typically done with a figure similar to Figure 4.1. As you can see, environmental impact peaks and then decreases while economic output keeps growing. This is the promise of decoupling. We get to have economic growth while reducing environmental impact to sustainable levels – levels that don't cause unacceptable environmental damages. The axes in these figures tend to be unlabeled, which means there is no sense of the time frame or the level of eco-efficiency gains required to bend the curve in such a way. A WBCSD learning module on eco-efficiency from 2006 shows more or less the exact same figure on the first page of its first chapter called "What is eco-efficiency?"[14]

We have already seen that in the critically important case of CO_2 emissions the environmental impact reductions achieved since Rio fell woefully short of the aspirations depicted in Figure 4.1. Figure 4.2 shows the actual decoupling that happened between global GDP and global CO_2 emissions since 1960. Unfortunately, CO_2 emissions have not peaked and decreased. Instead, they grew 62% between 1992 and 2019. CO_2 emissions still decoupled from economic growth; in other words, they grew more slowly than GDP. Some people call this 'relative decoupling' in order to distinguish it from Figure 4.1, which they would call 'absolute decoupling'. Obviously, growing more slowly than GDP is no use when the objective is to decrease in absolute terms or, as is the case with CO_2 emissions, reach net zero by 2050.[15]

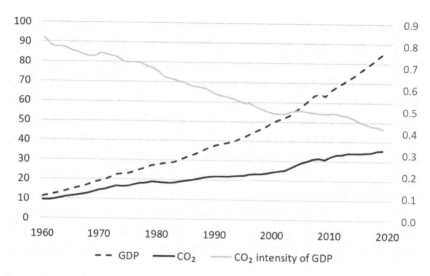

Figure 4.2 Actual decoupling between global GDP (in trillion 2010 USD) and CO_2 emissions from fossil fuel combustion and cement production (in billion tons)[16]

Figure 4.2 also depicts the eco-efficiency indicator you obtain when you divide the CO_2 emissions of any given year by that year's GDP. The indicator is called the CO_2 intensity of global GDP and shown here in kg CO_2 per 2010 USD. It decreased from 0.79 in 1962 to 0.56 in 1992 and 0.42 in 2019. On its own, this looks like a success story, which, of course, it isn't. By keeping one's sights trained narrowly on eco-efficiency gains, one runs the risk of missing the actual goal, which is moving the planet from its unsustainable pathway. Instead of seeing that, since the Earth Summit, global CO_2 emissions have increased by 62%, eco-efficiency advocates would spread the good news that CO_2 intensity of GDP has gone down by 25%. That, in a nutshell, is the problem with eco-efficiency.

Let's briefly revisit the issue of energy consumption and energy efficiency that we started this chapter with. As you may have guessed, all our energy efficiency efforts since the Earth Summit and before did not manage to arrest the growth in global energy consumption. According to BP's energy report, global energy consumption went from 347 Exajoules in 1992 to 584 in 2019 (there are a few more than 4,000 Joules in a food calorie, and 'exa' stands for 10 to the power of 18 or a billion billion).[17] During the same period, energy intensity of global GDP, another eco-efficiency

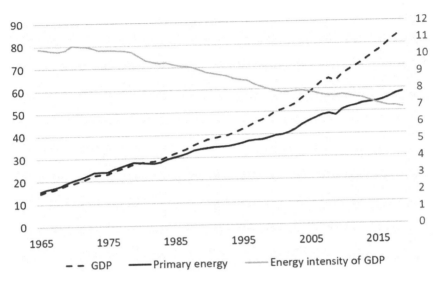

Figure 4.3 Actual decoupling between global GDP (in trillion 2010 USD) and primary energy consumption (in 10^{19} Joules)[19]

indicator, dropped from 8.9 megajoules per 2010 USD to 6.9, a 23% reduction (mega stands for one million). The 23% reduction in the energy intensity of global GDP since Rio is right in line with the 25% reduction of its CO_2 intensity. This is unsurprising since fossil fuels still make up 84% of the global energy mix, and their combustion is the main source of anthropogenic CO_2 emissions.[18] Figure 4.3 shows economic growth and energy consumption since 1965. We can see that total energy use has deftly outgrown our energy efficiency gains over the last fifty-five years.

As mentioned earlier, right around the Earth Summit and the publication of "Changing Course" the narrative around business and the environment changed dramatically from one of fighting environmental regulation and activism to one of opportunity and shared interests. This paradigm shift generated the current thinking about business and the environment, frequently called corporate sustainability or corporate environmental management. The idea that business and environmental protection could be synergistic rather than antagonistic quickly spread across industry, government, and academia, including business schools. One pertinent example was the inauguration of the Sandoz Chair in Management and the Environment in 1992 at INSEAD, a leading business school located 60 kilometers south of Paris. The chair was awarded to Robert Ayres, who six years later had the kindness to accept me as a researcher even though I had no formal qualification in environmental management whatsoever. Since my graduation from university in 1997, I had been looking for jobs in the new emerging area of corporate sustainability but was always told I lacked the necessary qualifications. It made no difference when I explained that, when I entered university, there were no degrees or courses in this area since it simply didn't exist back then.

Eco-efficiency and win-win were, and still are, central elements of the then emerging field of corporate environmental management. According to the WBCSD, "eco-efficiency [. . .] allows companies to become more environmentally responsible and profitable. Not only can it save production cost but can also open up new sources of revenue for companies."[20] I have sympathy for the apparent need to will these beliefs into being. Business schools are in the business of teaching and researching how firms can be more successful. Successful essentially means financially successful. In my own experience, talking at business schools about environmental impact reduction for its own sake is a nonstarter. But boldly claim that being green is a new way to reduce costs and increase revenues, and you pique business school people's interest.

The dominance of eco-efficiency is not limited to business schools. It has become the main, if not sole, way everyone studies, measures, and discusses the relationship between business and the environment. Another research area that emerged in the late 1980s and early 1990s is called industrial ecology, which studies the flows of materials and energy in industrial and consumer activities and the effects of these flows on the environment. The focus on physical rather than monetary flows attracts engineers and physicists like Bob Ayres and me, yet even industrial ecology is dominated by the narrative of eco-efficiency and win-win. Industrial ecology generated much of the research on decoupling and its best-known tool, life cycle assessment (LCA), takes a pure eco-efficiency approach by quantifying environmental impact per unit of product or service. LCAs quantify the environmental impacts of a car, a fridge, a piece of clothing, a kilogram of a certain material, or one kilowatt hour of electricity.

In 2016, I was invited by one of the main LCA consultancies to present a lunchtime webinar, or brown bag presentation as they are called in the United States, to talk about a recent publication called "There is no such thing as a green product" that I wrote with my former PhD student and now colleague Trevor Zink. In it, we discuss the risks of focusing exclusively on environmental impact per unit product or service, as LCA does, while ignoring the broader context, such as changes in total market and consumer behavior. What good was it to halve the impact of making a certain material when total production of it doubles in the meantime? Or doubling the energy efficiency of a product when people end up using it twice as much? The technical director of the consultancy was deeply unimpressed by my talk. He thought that a) it was very unlikely that something like that would happen and b) it was simply not the job of LCA practitioners to think about these fuzzy big-picture issues. Instead, their job was to quantify the life cycle impacts of a unit of product or service. With this information, their client could a) look for ways to increase the greenness of their product or service and b) benchmark it against alternatives.

And this is pretty much what happens in the world of corporate sustainability. The sustainability report of a beverage company may report that an externally conducted and verified LCA shows that their change in bottle material or design reduced its carbon footprint by 10%, 15%, or 20% per bottle. But the same company may have a financial report that proudly informs investors that sales have doubled since they switched containers. Most companies, including their sustainability managers, seem to have no apparent awareness of this dilemma.

The question whether, historically, efficiency improvements of products and services where outpaced by their growth in consumption is the subject of a seminal paper by Jeffrey Dahmus, which deservedly won the 2014 Journal of Industrial Ecology Senior Author Best Paper Prize. Dahmus studied ten different products and services. They are: Motor vehicle, passenger air, and freight rail travel; electricity generation from coal, oil, and natural gas; residential refrigeration; and nitrogen fertilizer, aluminum, and pig iron production. In case you wonder, pig iron is an intermediate product in steel production. It comes out of the smelting furnace but has too much carbon content to be useful without subsequent carbon removal.

Dahmus painstakingly collected data on annual production output and energy input for all ten activities over long time periods, ranging from five to eighteen decades. In every single case, the energy efficiency increased, frequently by a factor of two or three. In the case of pig iron production, energy efficiency increased 13-fold over a period of 180 years. And in every single case, growth in output outpaced the efficiency gains so that total energy consumption increased. Or as Dahmus says in his publication: "Historically, over long time periods, incremental improvements in efficiency have not succeeded in outpacing increases in the quantity of goods and services provided."[21] That is the problem with the reduction of corporate environmental management to the study and pursuit of eco-efficiency.

The data collected by Dahmus shows year-by-year changes in total output and energy efficiency and thus enables much more detailed analysis. It shows that efficiency gains can be quite uneven, accelerate at times, and level off at others. Dahmus notes that price pressures, efficiency mandates, and industry upheavals appear to impact efficiency. The data also shows that there can be periods in which efficiency gains reduce total energy consumption. The most encouraging case in his study is residential refrigeration. According to his data, total electricity consumption of U.S. residential refrigeration peaked in 1984 and has been declining until 2009, when the data ends. Absolute decoupling, the holy grail of eco-efficiency, has been achieved, at least for a while.

So, I don't want you to leave this chapter thinking that I consider the pursuit of energy efficiency, or eco-efficiency more broadly, to be useless. Instead, I am just warning that reducing corporate sustainability efforts to the single-minded pursuit of eco-efficiency dangerously narrows one's perspective. In the best case, such narrow focus takes everyone's eye off the real objective, which is to reduce total impact. In the worst case, efficiency gains may actually be drivers for growth and thus total impact and therefore tragically contain their own undoing. An LCA comparing Watt's and Newcomen's steam engine would have come to the conclusion that Watt's design is a green innovation of the highest order. It would not have informed us that it would also propel the industrial revolution into high gear.

Notes

1   William Stanley Jevons, "Of the Economy of Fuel," in *The Coal Question; An Inquiry Concerning the Progress of the Nation, and the Probable Exhaustion of Our Coal-Mines* (London and Cambridge: MacMillan and Co., 1865), https://doi.org/10.1177%2F1086026601141005.

2   Harry D. Saunders, "The Khazzoom-Brookes Postulate and Neoclassical Growth," *The Energy Journal* 13, no. 4 (1992), accessed July 21, 2020, www.jstor.org/stable/41322471.

3   Sheetal Gavankar and Roland Geyer, "The Rebound Effect: State of the Debate and Implications for Energy Efficiency Research," *The Bren School of Environmental Science and Management*, (2010); Steve Sorrell, John Dimitropoulos, and Matt Sommerville, "Empirical Estimates of the Direct Rebound Effect: A Review," *Energy Policy* 37, no. 4 (2009): pp. 1356–1371, accessed July 21, 2020, https://doi.org/10.1016/j.enpol.2008.11.026.

4   Bente Halvorsen and Bodil Merethe Larsen, "How Do Investments in Heat Pumps Affect Household Energy Consumption?," *Discussion Papers: Statistics Norway Research Department*, no. 737 (April 2013), accessed July 21, 2020, www.ssb.no/nasjonalregnskap-og-konjunkturer/artikler-og-publikasjoner/_attachment/109798?_ts=13e3ae9f3f8.

5   Bente Halvorsen and Bodil Merethe Larsen, "How Do Investments in Heat Pumps Affect Household Energy Consumption?," *Discussion Papers: Statistics Norway Research Department*, no. 737 (April 2013), accessed July 21, 2020, www.ssb.no/nasjonalregnskap-og-konjunkturer/artikler-og-publikasjoner/_attachment/109798?_ts=13e3ae9f3f8.

6   Sheetal Gavankar and Roland Geyer, "The Rebound Effect: State of the Debate and Implications for Energy Efficiency Research," *The Bren School of Environmental Science and Management*, (2010); Angela Druckman, Mona Chitnis, Steve Sorrell, and Tim Jackson, "Missing Carbon Reductions? Exploring Rebound and Backfire Effects in UK Households," *Energy Policy* 39 (2011): pp. 3572–3581, accessed January 3, 2021, https://doi.org/10.1016/j.enpol.2011.03.058.

7   Harry D. Saunders, "The Khazzoom-Brookes Postulate and Neoclassical Growth," *The Energy Journal* 13, no. 4 (1992), accessed July 21, 2020, www.iaee.org/energyjournal/article/1091.

8   "Stephan Schmidheiny," accessed July 21, 2020, www.stephanschmidheiny.com/en/science/.

9   "Stephan Schmidheiny," accessed July 21, 2020, www.stephanschmidheiny.com/en/science/.

10 Michael E. Porter, "America's Green Strategy," *Scientific American* 264, no. 4 (April 1991), accessed January 13, 2021, www.scientificamerican.com/article/essay-1991-04/; Michael E. Porter and Claas Van der Linde, "Toward a New Conception of the Environment-Competitiveness Relationship," *Journal of Economic Perspectives* 9, no. 4 (1995): pp. 97–118, accessed July 21, 2020, www.jstor.org/stable/2138392.

11   "Report of the World Commission on Environment and Development: Our Common Future," *United Nations*, (1987), accessed July 21, 2020, https://sustainabledevelopment.un.org/content/documents/5987our-common-future.pdf.

12   "GDP (Constant 2010 USD)," *The World Bank*, accessed January 13, 2021, https://data.worldbank.org/indicator/NY.GDP.MKTP.KD; "Statistical Review of World Energy 2020," *British Petroleum*, (2020), accessed January 13, 2021, www.bp.com/en/global/corporate/energy-economics/statistical-review-of-world-energy.html;

    Robbie M. Andrew, "Global CO2 Emissions from Cement Production, 1928–2018," *CICERO Center for International Climate Research*, (2019), accessed January 13, 2021, https://essd.copernicus.org/preprints/essd-2019-152/essd-2019-152.pdf.

13   "Our History," *The World Business Council on Sustainable Development*, accessed July 21, 2020, www.wbcsd.org/Overview/Our-history.

14   Katherine Madden, Rebekah Young, Kevin Brady, and Jennifer Hall, "Eco-efficiency: Learning Module," *The World Business Council on Sustainable Development*, last modified August 24, 2006, accessed July 21, 2020, www.wbcsd.org/Projects/Education/Resources/Eco-efficiency-Learning-Module.

15   According to the UN IPCC, limiting warming to 1.5°C would require global net human-caused CO2 emissions to fall by about 45 percent from 2010 levels by 2030, reaching 'net zero' around 2050;
"Climate Action: Key Findings," *United Nations*, accessed January 13, 2021, www.un.org/en/climatechange/science/key-findings.

16   "GDP (Constant 2010 USD)," *The World Bank*, accessed January 13, 2021, https://data.worldbank.org/indicator/NY.GDP.MKTP.KD; "Statistical Review of World Energy 2020," *British Petroleum*, (2020), accessed January 13, 2021, www.bp.com/en/global/corporate/energy-economics/statistical-review-of-world-energy.html;

    Robbie M. Andrew, "Global CO2 Emissions from Cement Production, 1928–2018," *CICERO Center for International Climate Research*, (2019), accessed January 13, 2021, https://essd.copernicus.org/preprints/essd-2019-152/essd-2019-152.pdf.

17   "Statistical Review of World Energy 2020," *British Petroleum*, (2020), accessed January 6, 2021, www.bp.com/en/global/corporate/energy-economics/statistical-review-of-world-energy.html.

18 "Statistical Review of World Energy 2020," *British Petroleum*, (2020), accessed January 6, 2021, www.bp.com/en/global/corporate/energy-economics/statistical-review-of-world-energy.html.

19 "GDP (Constant 2010 USD)," *The World* Bank, accessed January 13, 2021, https://data.worldbank.org/indicator/NY.GDP.MKTP.KD; "Statistical Review of World Energy 2020," *British Petroleum*, (2020), accessed January 13, 2021, www.bp.com/en/global/corporate/energy-economics/statistical-review-of-world-energy.html;

Robbie M. Andrew, "Global CO2 Emissions from Cement Production, 1928–2018," *CICERO Center for International Climate Research*, (2019), accessed January 13, 2021, https://essd.copernicus.org/preprints/essd-2019-152/essd-2019-152.pdf.

20 "Our History," *The World Business Council on Sustainable Development*, accessed July 21, 2020, www.wbcsd.org/Overview/Our-history.

21 Jeffrey B. Dahmus, "Can Efficiency Improvements Reduce Resource Consumption? A Historical Analysis of Ten Activities," *Journal of Industrial Ecology* 18, no. 6 (2014): pp. 883–897, accessed July 21, 2020, https://doi.org/10.1111/jiec.12110.

5

WHY WIN-WIN WON'T WORK

The win-win paradigm is so pervasive in corporate sustainability that questioning it is a bit like questioning gravity. Despite early doubts, it took me the better part of twenty years to build up the courage to do so. It all started with cell phone reuse. It was 1999, and I was working with Bob Ayres and Luk van Wassenhove at INSEAD, one of Europe's leading business schools. I introduced Bob in the previous chapter on eco-efficiency. Luk is a distinguished professor of supply chain management and was my second mentor at INSEAD. Both professors were kind enough to take me under their wings despite my distinct lack of environmental or supply chain expertise. The task I was given was to study the economics of product reuse, also called refurbishment or remanufacturing.[1] Everyone took the environmental benefits of reuse as a given. The question was how to turn it into an attractive business proposition; after all, that's what business schools are all about. One of the few examples of reuse happening in the real world was cell phone refurbishment. Small companies, like ReCellular in the U.S. and Greener Solutions in the UK, would collect used handsets, test them,

DOI:10.4324/9781003163060-05

do some basic repair and refurbishment, and resell them. These companies were seen and praised as sustainability role models, and the idea was to learn how their business models could be applied to other products and industries.

One puzzling aspect of cell phone refurbishment was that it was supported by some producers of new handsets, like Motorola, but opposed by others, such as Nokia. We suspected that it came down to their differing beliefs about cannibalization. Cannibalization is marketing speak and refers to a reduction in product sales caused by the introduction of similar products, since customers start buying the new model instead of the existing one. We knew that managers at Motorola were certain that refurbished handsets did not cannibalize new phone sales and instead just opened up new markets. We also suspected that Nokia believed the opposite and thus saw refurbished phones as unwelcome competitors. To avoid the wrath of new product manufacturers, third-party refurbishers had to assure them that refurbished products did not cannibalize new product sales. This was the case with Motorola, who actually encouraged its customers to return their old handsets to ReCellular. Unfortunately, I had convinced myself that the only environmental benefit of product reuse (refurbishment, remanufacturing, etc.) comes from avoiding the production of new products. In other words, cannibalization is bad for business but good for the environment. An inherent and irreconcilable dichotomy seemed to be at the core of the win-win paradigm, at least in the case of remanufacturing. I seemed to be the only one at INSEAD who was alarmed by this.

As we have discussed in Chapter 2, the idea that pollution prevention can generate cost savings goes back to the mid-1970s when 3M started its Pollution Prevention Pays (3P) program. It challenged the consensus view of the time that business and the environment were fundamentally at odds. Over the next two decades, this new narrative morphed into the win-win paradigm, which claimed that opportunities in which environmental and business benefits coincide are widespread and should thus be seen as a major avenue towards environmental sustainability. The win-win rhetoric was so successful that by the end of the 1990s, win-win started to be seen as the only way to reconcile business and the environment, since companies require the economic win as incentive to act due to the primacy of shareholder value. This was the ethos I encountered when I joined INSEAD as a researcher. Business schools brimmed with win-win enthusiasm, and sustainability was suddenly a hot topic for them. It did appear that most business scholars and students saw win-win as just another way to identify business opportunities, with the added bonus of 'doing well by doing good'. But then who wouldn't like to make a ton of money while saving the environment?

The win-win paradigm had plenty of critics right from the beginning, but there was no one who questioned the desirability of win-win opportunities. Instead, the critics questioned their abundance. A pertinent example is the Harvard Business Review (HBR) article by McKinsey consultants Walley and Whitehead, which was mentioned in Chapter 2 and from which the title of this chapter is stolen (reused?). In Walley and Whitehead's view, win-win won't work because there simply aren't enough win-win opportunities to make a big difference.[2] The win-win pessimists were criticized, in turn, by win-win optimists who maintained that, yes indeed, win-win opportunities were plentiful. Win-win enthusiasts Porter and van der Linde went as far as saying that pollution is just a form of inefficiency.[3] The debate about the abundance of win-win opportunities has been raging ever since and, to my knowledge, has never been settled. Instead, a kind of discussion fatigue set in after a while, and business and other scholars have simply moved on to other research topics. Yet, to this day, no one argues that win-win is the best way, probably the only way, to interest the business community in environmental activities that go beyond mere compliance with environmental regulation. In other words, corporate sustainability and win-win are more or less synonymous. While eco-efficiency is supposed to reconcile continued economic growth with environmental impact reduction, win-win is meant to provide the incentive for companies to look for impact reduction opportunities.

What if the trouble with win-win is not that there might be a lack of win-win opportunities but rather that it simply doesn't work as a mechanism? I have come to the conclusion that it doesn't and will use the rest of this chapter to explain why.

Let's start with an example that may appear a bit silly initially, until we realize that it's not. Here it is: A shoe company with a reputation for caring about the environment had a radical technological breakthrough that enables it to produce its most popular model not only for half the cost but also with half the environmental impact. The company is privately held, and the owners decide to pass on the entire cost savings to its customers by slashing the price of said shoe model in half. Customers are ecstatic about the incredible reductions in both price and environmental impact. In no time at all, sales of that now very green shoe model double.

Let's dissect what just happened. Environmental impact per pair of shoes went down by 50%, a veritable eco-efficiency triumph. Production cost of a pair of shoes also went down by 50%, creating a win-win of the highest order. Despite the apparent selflessness of the company's owners, revenue and profit from this particular shoe model stayed the same, thanks to the doubling in sales. Customers have now twice as many of their favorite green shoes. The only fly in the ointment is that the environmental impact from that shoe model hasn't changed one bit. The impact per pair of shoes has halved, but the total environmental impact is the same. The impact reduction per pair of shoes was eaten up completely by the doubling in shoe production and sales.

I am all but certain that you would like to raise multiple objections at this point. I will attempt to address all of them. Maybe the most obvious issue you might take with the green shoe example is the assumption that shoe sales double after their price was cut in half. Who needs that many shoes? It turns out that the doubling shoe sales assumption is unnecessary for the argument. Let's assume that before the win-win breakthrough, the price of a pair was $100 and annual sales were 100,000, creating annual revenues of $10 million. Let's further assume sales stayed constant, even after the price dropped to $50. This means that households have cost savings of $5 million, while still getting the exact same number of shoes. If the households don't spend the cost savings on shoes, they are going to spend it on other things, which have their own environmental impacts.

Let's assume that, before the win-win breakthrough, producing one pair of shoes generated 14 kilogram (kg) of greenhouse gas (GHG) emissions (measured in CO_2 equivalent or CO_2e).[4]

The GHG intensity of shoe production, before and after the breakthrough, is therefore 0.14 kg CO_2e per dollar (14 kg CO_2e / $100 and 7 kg CO_2e / $50). If annual shoe sales stay at 100,000 after breakthrough, total GHG emissions from shoe production drop from 1.4 million kg CO_2e to 0.7 million. But households now have $5 million to spend on other things. If the GHG intensity of all those other goods and services households buy with their $5 million is also 0.14 kg CO_2e per dollar, the total GHG emissions of these purchases add up to 0.7 million kg CO_2e. So, all that happened is that the win-win breakthrough of the shoe company shifted GHG emissions from shoes to other products. If all of this reminds you of the indirect rebound effect described in the previous chapter, you're not mistaken. That is the essence of what just happened here.

The next objection many of you would now rightfully raise is the assumption that the shoe company would pass along the entire cost savings to its customers. It turns out that this assumption is also not required to challenge the win-win paradigm. Let's instead assume that the company leaves the price of the shoes unchanged and pockets all cost savings as additional profit. Well, these additional profits turn into additional shareholder income and will thus simply be spent by different households. If we again assume that the GHG intensity of household spending is 0.14 kg CO_2e per dollar, the GHG emissions of the shoe company customers goes down by 0.7 million kg, while the GHG emissions of the shoe company shareholders goes up by 0.7 million kg. All that the win-win opportunity did in this case was shift GHG emissions from one part of the population to another.

But hold on a minute, you may say, we're assuming that all cost savings are immediately spent again. How realistic is that? Fairly, it turns out. In many countries, the saving rate – the fraction of disposable income saved rather than spent – is in the single digits. For almost all countries, the saving rate is below 15%.[5] So, most of the cost savings of this hypothetical win-win case study would indeed be spent instead of saved. More importantly, though, it is irrelevant whether they would be spent or saved. Saving money just means that the spending is postponed to the future. If the future GHG intensity is 0.14 kg of CO_2e per saved dollar, we end up with the exact same total environmental impact. In this case, all the win-win opportunity did was to spread out the GHG emissions over time. Now, to exactly evaluate the environmental difference between spending money today versus saving it for a while and then spending it is complicated. We would have to consider the saving interest rate, inflation, the future GHG intensity of household spending, and even the question whether simply delaying GHG emissions has an environmental value in and of itself. All true, but the bottom line is that all cost savings from win-win opportunities will be spent by someone, somewhere, sometime and thus generate their own environmental impacts, whatever their exact size might be. The win-win paradigm works like a magic trick. It makes environmental impact disappear, while, in fact, it simply moved it to a place where you can't see it directly.

I can think of yet another objection to the reasoning presented so far. What if the cost savings from a win-win opportunity are reinvested rather than spent or saved? To this, I would say that reinvesting the cost savings is almost guaranteed to increase total environmental impact rather than reduce it. The simple reason for this is that investments are designed to yield returns and grow a business, or more generally, the economy. So are savings by the way. Your savings are someone else's loan, which has to be paid back with interest and therefore better yield returns that are higher than the interest. There is just no way around it: Win-win is not the right mechanism to achieve significant environmental impact reductions. The only way to guarantee that the cost savings of a win-win don't undo the initial environmental impact reductions is to make sure those economic savings are never turned into environmental impact. In other words, the economic savings must not be spent on, saved for, or invested in products or services with environmental impact. That would mean that it's not a win-win in the original sense anymore.

So, where does that leave us? It means that the win-win paradigm is not the right mechanism for incentivizing businesses to look for ways to reduce environmental impact. We urgently need to find better incentives for beyond compliance environmental business behavior. By the way, I am far from being the first or the only person to say this. In 1998, Professors Tim Jackson and Roland Clift published a short essay with similar sentiments and arguments. Reading it convinced me to seek them out as my PhD advisors. The essay is only three pages long and called "Where's the Profit in Industrial Ecology?"[6] It appeared in the first issue of the second volume of the then still very new Journal of Industrial Ecology.

As I mentioned in the previous chapter on eco-efficiency, the entire field of industrial ecology was very new back then. Like the field of economics, industrial ecology studies systems of production and consumption, but unlike economics it doesn't exclusively focus on the monetary flows, like costs and revenues. Instead, it studies the material and energy flows in production and consumption activities. To a physicist with a passion for environmental sustainability like me, this made immediate sense. How else can we understand the environmental impacts of businesses and the economy at large? As fellow physicist Bob Ayres, who is considered one of the founding fathers of industrial ecology, once told me: Only economists can make bread with nothing but capital and labor; everyone else needs flour, water, an oven, and so on. So I decided to become an industrial ecologist, while not forgetting the important insights I gleaned from my stint at a high-powered business school like INSEAD.

In their 1998 article, Jackson and Clift point out that industrial ecologists have a tendency to look for opportunities to reduce environmental impacts in our production and consumption systems without considering who should implement them and why. Industrial ecology thus lacks an explicit 'theory of agency'. However, Jackson and Clift continue, at closer inspection we see that industrial ecologists consistently point out that many of the identified environmental impact reduction opportunities are good for profitability, either by reducing cost, increasing revenues, or both. The implicit theory of agency underlying industrial ecology is thus the profit motive, which constitutes a quiet, and somewhat coy, embrace of the win-win paradigm.

Next, Jackson and Clift assure the reader that there are indeed many opportunities to reduce environmental impact that also reduce cost, such as reducing waste, using energy and materials more efficiently, and reusing and recycling more. Yet, while the profit motive makes businesses look for cost-saving opportunities to make production more efficient, it also makes them look for ways to increase their revenues by selling more stuff. More stuff equals more environmental impact. Jackson and Clift call this "an almost irresolvable tension at the heart of industrial ecology" and end the article by encouraging the readers to look for alternative theories of agency.[7] The article had a huge impact on me but apparently not on many other industrial ecologists. In the twenty years since its publication, the essay was cited a measly 88 times. In 2008, I was a few years into my tenure-track assistant professorship and finally submitted my doubts about the assumed environmental benefits of cell phone refurbishment to the Journal of Industrial Ecology, the same journal that had published the piece by Jackson and Clift ten years before. The reviews of my manuscript were so negative that I eventually gave up on trying to publish it. I can still see it in limbo in the online submission system of the journal every time I log on.

According to Jackson and Clift, the win-win paradigm "is driving us in two conflicting directions": "toward improved production efficiency" on one hand and "toward increased production output" on the other.[8] We have seen, in the previous chapter, how growth in global output has consistently exceeded improvements in production efficiency, which is why global energy consumption and CO_2 emissions keep rising, along with many other environmental impact indicators. This is the empty promise of eco-efficiency. However, our hypothetical shoe production case study suggests that the win-win paradigm is flawed in an even more fundamental and irredeemable way, since the cost savings of improved production efficiencies shift environmental impact through rebound effects rather than truly reduce it. Win-win won't work, one way or the other.

Saying that something has a rebound effect is just a way of admitting that the scope of the original analysis was too narrow, that something potentially important was left out. So, the scope created by the eco-efficiency concept and the win-win paradigm is too small to capture all important environmental implications. This is why the narrow focus on eco-efficiency and win-win used by most, if not all, corporate sustainability efforts did not deliver the hoped-for (and desperately needed) reductions in total environmental impact. By definition, increasing eco-efficiency decreases the environmental impact per product or per dollar of production. However, as discussed in the previous chapter, increasing eco-efficiency is also almost certain to effect changes in consumer behavior, product markets, or the economy as a whole, which dampen or even eliminate the apparent impact reductions. Similarly, implementing a win-win opportunity, by definition, generates environmental and economic benefits. Traditional analysis of a win-win ignores that the economic benefits generate their own environmental impacts, which have to be subtracted from the original environmental benefits to obtain the net environmental effect. I have chosen the numbers in the shoe case study so that the environmental impact of spending the cost savings, either by the customers or the shareholders, completely eliminates the environmental impact reductions during shoe production. In real world examples, the environmental impact generated by the economic benefits could, of course, be smaller, equal, or greater than the direct impact reductions. Existing estimates of the carbon intensity of marginal household spending are actually higher than the 0.14 kg CO_2e per dollar I used for shoe production.[9] This means that the win-win in our shoe case study would lead to an increase in environmental impact. To estimate the net environmental effect of an environmental business or consumer activity requires an appropriately scoped assessment. What this looks like is the subject of the next chapter.

What is the best way to minimize the undesired environmental impacts generated by win-win's economic benefits? By not having any economic benefits in the first place, that is, by doing away with the demand that business activities designed to reduce environmental impacts need to generate significant economic benefits as well in order to even be considered. Imagine that the shoe company in our case study had found and implemented a technological breakthrough that halved the environmental impact of shoe production at the original cost rather than lower cost. The environmental impact of shoe production would still go down by 50%, but everything else would stay the same. No rebound effects, neither direct nor indirect nor economy-wide. As one of my PhD students pointed out to me recently, there is something slightly nonsensical about the win-win paradigm as a necessary catalyst for environmental action. We want that businesses (and households) voluntarily look for and implement opportunities to reduce their environmental impacts. Yet we also assume that they will only act if those opportunities are very much in their economic self-interest. But if that is the case, then their behavior is not really environmental, is it? It's simply self-interested economic behavior that would happen anyway, environmental benefits or not. Apparently, we think that we have to trick businesses and households into environmental action; like tricking children into eating healthy food instead of teaching them to love healthy food and eat it voluntarily and on purpose. But the businesses and households we're trying to trick, that's us. Each one of us is a member of a household, and many of us are part of a business. If we truly think that we can't be asked to reduce our environmental impacts simply for the sake of avoiding climate catastrophe, mass extinction, and a whole host of other environmental perils, then we should just admit to the fundamental futility of the whole enterprise and stop fooling ourselves. That would be a lot more honest than keep on chasing the rainbow unicorns of eco-efficiency and win-win as sole tools to reconcile business and the environment and then be surprised that it doesn't work.

One possible reason why the win-win paradigm is so dominant in all discussions about business and the environment is that having a viable business and constantly seeking to increase revenues and profits is seen as one and the same thing. Maybe it's because I'm trained as a physicist rather than an economist or business scholar, but I just can't see why that should be. I have always struggled with the axiomatic assumptions that businesses are profit maximizers and consumers maximize this elusive quantity called utility. As it turns out, economists simply borrowed the maximization principle from 19th century classical mechanics without thinking too hard about the implications or trying to validate the resulting theories with empirical evidence.[10] Unfortunately, the assumption of profit and utility maximization still appears to be standard in economics and particularly in management science.

That businesses are profit-maximizing entities seems more like a self-fulfilling prophecy to me. We told ourselves long enough that this is how business works, so now it seems to work like this. In an influential essay in the New York Times Magazine in 1970, famous economist Milton Friedman simply states that the owners, or shareholders, of businesses want to make as much money as possible. He then concludes that "the social responsibility of business is to increase its profits."[11] In the essay, Friedman derides businessmen who "declaim that business is not concerned 'merely' with profit but also with promoting 'social' ends." Pursuing anything but profit maximization would violate the responsibility of business managers to their shareholders. Friedman's argumentation seems to switch freely between the descriptive and the normative, which is remarkable for someone who frequently lamented lack of rigor. Friedman is one of the best-known faces of the so-called Chicago School of Economics or neo-classical economics more broadly. He and his colleagues were so successful in persuading everyone that increasing shareholder value is the only purpose of business that no self-respecting business scholar or manager dares to question it. Until now, that is.

In summer of 2019, the Business Roundtable, a lobbying organization made up of the CEOs from nearly 200 of America's largest companies, announced that it would change its official doctrine from 1997, which states that "the paramount duty of management [. . .] is to the corporation's stockholders."[12] According to the announcement, the purpose of a business should go beyond shareholder value and consider all other stakeholders, including the environment. The CEOs from the Business Roundtable sound very much like those businessmen in the late 1960s that Friedman ridiculed and chided. It looks like we have come full circle during the last fifty years of business and the environment. It is possible, of course, that these proclamations of social responsibility were then and are now mere lip service. Friedman suspected as much and indeed hoped it was. But even if it is, it is still remarkable that CEOs think that they have to publicly embrace social responsibility (again). In essence, the Business Roundtable just said "yes, we need to make money, but that is not everything." It is no coincidence that the last ten years also saw the birth and rise of the 'benefit corporation', which explicitly includes positive impacts on society, workers, the community, and the environment as its legally defined goals in addition to profit. Who knows; maybe we are witnessing the beginning of the end of profit maximization?

Since I'm already questioning economic motherhood and apple pie, I might as well go completely off the neo-classical rails. I argued earlier that the best way to avoid the unintended (and presumably undesired) environmental consequences of win-win is to not have any economic benefits. In other words, let's not require that opportunities for environmental impact reduction also reduce cost. Is there a way to not just avoid rebound effects but even further add to the original environmental impact reduction? Indeed. Implement environmental impact reduction opportunities that are costlier than the status quo. Such a cost increase will create a rebound effect that adds to, rather than subtracts from, the original environmental benefits. One could call it a reverse rebound effect. Imagine that the shoe company in our case study had found and implemented a technological breakthrough that halved the environmental impact of shoe production at slightly higher cost than the original, say $10 more per pair of shoes. There are two things the company can do: It can either pass on the additional cost to its customers and now charge $110 for a pair of green shoes, or it can absorb the additional cost and accept a lower profit margin. Sound impossible? The latter is exactly what happened when apparel company Patagonia switched its entire product portfolio from conventional to organic cotton in 1997 and absorbed the cost increase. Back to the fictional shoe company. If shoe sales remain the same, the total additional cost of $1 million is now no longer available to spend, either by the company's shareholders or customers. This further reduces environmental impact. A different kind of win-win, one could say.

How realistic is this? To be honest, I don't know. Consumers consistently state that they are willing to pay price premiums for green products but then tend to not do so when they actually go shopping. More and more companies are talking about their social responsibility (again), and fewer and fewer people actually believe them. Nevertheless, I have come to the conclusion that we need to treat reduced environmental impact as a valuable and desirable product attribute, not some deficiency that requires a cost/price reduction to sway managers/customers to make/buy the product. Maybe we need to start a new self-fulfilling prophecy. One that says that companies and customers care for environmental benefits for their own sake and are therefore willing to pay for them. I actually think it would work; I'm just worried that it might take too long, since we don't have another fifty years for it to take hold.

Notes

1   Roland Geyer and Vered Blass, "The Economics of Cell Phone Reuse and Recycling," *The International Journal of Advanced Manufacturing Technology* 47, nos. 5–8 (2010): pp. 515–525, accessed January 13, 2021, https://doi.org/10.1007/s00170-009-2228-z.

2   Noah Walley and Bradley Whitehead, "It's Not Easy Being Green," *Harvard Business Review* 72, no. 3 (May-June 1994): pp. 46–52, accessed January 13, 2021, https://hbr.org/1994/05/its-not-easy-being-green.

3   Michael E. Porter and Claas van der Linde, "Green and Competitive: Ending the Stalemate," *Harvard Business Review* 73, no. 5 (September–October 1995): pp. 120–134, accessed January 13, 2021, https://hbr.org/1995/09/green-and-competitive-ending-the-stalemate.

4   14 and 7 kg of CO_2e are realistic GHG values for shoe production. See, e.g., Lynette Cheah et al., "Manufacturing-focused Emissions Reductions in Footwear Production," *Journal of Cleaner Production* 44 (2013): pp. 18–29, accessed October 25, 2020, www.sciencedirect.com/science/article/abs/pii/S0959652612006300; "Sustainability," *Allbirds*, accessed October 25, 2020, www.allbirds.com/pages/sustainability.

5   "Gross Savings (% of GDP)," *The World Bank Group*, accessed July 21, 2020, https://data.worldbank.org/indicator/NY.GNS.ICTR.ZS.

6   Tim Jackson and Roland Clift, "Where's the Profit in Industrial Ecology?," *Journal of Industrial Ecology* 2, no. 1 (1998): pp. 3–5, accessed July 21, 2020, https://doi.org/10.1162/jiec.1998.2.1.3.

7   Tim Jackson and Roland Clift, "Where's the Profit in Industrial Ecology?," *Journal of Industrial Ecology* 2, no. 1 (1998): pp. 3–5, accessed July 21, 2020, https://doi.org/10.1162/jiec.1998.2.1.3.

8   Tim Jackson and Roland Clift, "Where's the Profit in Industrial Ecology?," *Journal of Industrial Ecology* 2, no. 1 (1998): pp. 3–5, accessed July 21, 2020, https://doi.org/10.1162/jiec.1998.2.1.3.

9   Tamar Makov and David Font Vivanco, "Does the Circular Economy Grow the Pie? The Case of Rebound Effects from Smartphone Reuse," *Frontiers in Energy Research* 6 (2018): p. 39, accessed October 25, 2020, https://doi.org/10.3389/fenrg.2018.00039.

10   Philip Mirkowski, *More Heat Than Light: Economics as Social Physics, Physics as Nature's Economics* (Cambridge, UK: Cambridge University Press, 1989).

11   Milton Friedman, "The Social Responsibility of Business Is to Increase Its Profits," *The New York Times Magazine*, last modified September 13, 1970, accessed January 13, 2021, http://umich.edu/~thecore/doc/Friedman.pdf.

12   David Gelles and David Yaffe-Bellany, "Shareholder Value Is No Longer Everything, Top C.E.O.s Say," *The New York Times*, last modified August 19, 2019, accessed January 13, 2021, www.nytimes.com/2019/08/19/business/business-roundtable-ceos-corporations.html.

6

THE BUSINESS OF LESS

I vividly remember reading Limits to Growth as a late teen. It is the mid-1980s, and I am on a lounger in my parents' garden in Northern Bavaria. It's a lazy summer afternoon, and insects are buzzing all around me. There are fruit trees to my left and rows of berries, vegetables, and herbs to my right: Raspberries, strawberries, gooseberries, red currant, black currant, all kinds of lettuce, zucchini, broccoli, cabbage, cauliflower, radishes, chives, parsley, dill, basil, tarragon. My parents were avid gardeners. The book is talking about global overshoot and collapse. Based on the reasoning presented by the authors, exponential growth versus a finite planet, it makes complete and utter sense. But how am I to reconcile these apocalyptic predictions with the Garden of Eden I am sitting in. And the dream of abundance I am living in, for that matter. West Germany, in the 1980s, was a seemingly never-ending feast of consumption and an endless procession of new products and technologies. Both my parents had lived through the Second World War and were frugal as a result. Yet even they were unable to withstand this conveyer belt of luxury goods and novelties turning into

DOI:10.4324/9781003163060-06

commodities: Sparkling wine, salmon, exotic fruit, power tools, appliances, reams of gadgets made of plastic, and later a whole slew of electronic equipment. I remember a game show in which the winning contestant was literally standing in front of a conveyer belt full of products moving past him. All he had to do was remember them after they had disappeared again, and they were his. This was Gordon Gekko's 'Greed is good' decade; I just didn't know it back then.[1]

There were reasons for my budding environmental awareness. The German Green Party had been formed a few years before and was now protesting against nuclear weapons, nuclear power, and environmental pollution. In most people's mind, the threat of nuclear disaster loomed larger than that of environmental pollution. A new generation of nuclear-capable ballistic missiles, Pershing II, was being deployed in Germany, causing demonstrations and civil disobedience. Two years after I discovered Limits to Growth, the core in Reactor 4 of the Chernobyl Nuclear Power Plant exploded. Good old-fashioned pollution, like acid rain, still managed to get some attention. Greenpeace activists were scaling smokestacks and unrolling banners to draw attention to the sudden tree die-offs in Germany's beloved forests, which gave the word 'Waldsterben' to the world. Yet, the Green Party and the Greenpeace activists were very much at the fringe of German society, which was mostly busy inventing new products and making and selling more of everything year over year. Worrying about global overshoot and collapse made me feel like a misfit, if not a failure, failing to want to be part of this march towards more products, more services, more wealth, more growth, more everything.

Now it is almost 2020, and I am sitting in a remote cabin above Carmel Valley in California. The last few years have been an endless procession of bad environmental news; I won't even try to summarize them. There seems to be a race on for which world region can melt the fastest: The Arctic, Greenland's ice, Siberia's permafrost, or Europe's glaciers. There also seems to be a race on for which animal population can decline the fastest: Insects in Germany, birds in the UK or the U.S., megafauna in Africa, or fish in the ocean. Every day we learn a new expression: Tipping points, extreme weather events, global weirding, mass extinction, climate crisis, climate emergency, climate breakdown. Time Magazine just named the sixteen-year-old climate activist Greta Thunberg person of the year. Even my father-in-law, who loves German luxury sedans and always seemed to believe that economic growth is the remedy to cure all ills, is talking about climate change, looking worried. A statement was published by 11,000 scientists this year, warning the world of 'untold suffering' unless we take swift and dramatic action.[2] Part of me wants to go back to the 1980s and tell everyone: I told you so! Fat lot of good that would do . . . I just wish I had had the confidence to write this book much earlier.

So this is where I find myself, where we find ourselves: A planet in peril. What is the role of business on a planet in peril? Is there one? There must be. Business is not going away. Business is how we make, move, and market all the goods and services we use every day. So the role of business on a planet in peril is to provide for everyone while dramatically reducing the environmental impact of doing so. This is what I call the business of less.

The business of less requires a compass to direct it towards actual environmental impact reduction. I argued, in the last two chapters, that eco-efficiency and win-win have set us on the wrong course for the last thirty years and thus need to be thrown overboard. This chapter presents an alternative. A few years ago, Trevor Zink and I came up with the idea and called it 'net green'. Back then, Trevor was a PhD student of mine. Today he is Associate Professor at the college of business administration at Loyola Marymount University in Los Angeles and a great colleague. The definition is so simple as to sound almost trivial:

A business activity is net green if it leads to an overall reduction in environmental impact.

The business activity in question can be any change in a business: Redesigning an existing product, launching a new product, changing suppliers, changing internal operations. The basic rationale behind net green is that any change in a business is likely to have multiple consequences, all of which might have significant environmental implications: some positive, some negative. Net environmental impact is the sum over all significant changes in environmental impact. The task at hand is thus to a) identify all consequences with significant environmental implications, b) quantify the environmental implications using a suitable environmental impact indicator, and c) sum up all the changes in impact in order to obtain the net change. This procedure is repeated if multiple impact indicators are warranted.

I will now illustrate the use of net green with the example of car sharing. Car sharing is the business model in which members can use cars on an hourly basis. Car sharing is different from car rental in that it is meant as an alternative to owning a car. Car sharing is also different from ridesharing since you drive yourself rather than be driven. Ridesharing companies like Uber and Lyft really just operate like taxis or shuttles rather than actually facilitating rideshares, but that's a different story. The car-sharing market is very dynamic. Current large players are Zipcar, Flinkster, and Share Now. The latter is the result of a 2018 merger between Daimler's car2go and BMW's DriveNow. Car sharing is just one example of the so-called sharing economy, which is about access to goods and services instead of ownership. As I mentioned in Chapter 3, selling services instead of selling products, which also goes by the terrible name servicizing, has been one of the mantras of industrial ecology and corporate environmental sustainability. Like reuse and recycling, it is typically considered to be green even without any real analysis. In Chapter 3, I also played devil's advocate by constructing a quantitative argument that appears to show that car sharing has the exact same environmental impacts as car ownership. We will now revisit car sharing and use net green analysis in order to assess its actual environmental performance.

Let's decide to use global warming potential, measured in kg CO_2e, as environmental impact indicator since there is an urgent need to reduce the greenhouse gas emissions from transportation. For cars and all other types of transportation, the majority of climate change impacts are caused by the use of the vehicles, not their production or disposal. For a car with an internal combustion engine, which is the one almost everyone currently drives, it's between 85% and 90% of total life cycle emissions.[3] The impact of transportation use is determined by the product between distance traveled and the efficiency of the transportation mode. Alternative and public transportation modes – think bike, bus, train – are typically much more efficient than cars.

The first step is to identify all relevant consequences of joining car sharing. There are four ways in which car sharing can change the transportation behavior of its users. First, joining a car-sharing service can lead a user to drive more or less than before. Second, the fuel efficiency of the shared cars can be higher or lower than the fuel efficiency of the cars used before joining the service. Third, the mix of used transportation modes can change as a result of joining a car-sharing service. The user might use more or less alternative and public transportation than before. Fourth, car sharing can affect the total amount of cars being produced. In fact, Zipcar claims that "each and every Zipcar takes 13 personally owned vehicles off the road."[4]

The next step in a net green analysis is to quantify the environmental impact of these four consequences in terms of direction and size. Luckily for us, a team of researchers at the University of California at Berkeley has studied many of the relevant questions, by asking over 6,000 car-sharing members how joining the service changed their travel behavior.[5] The survey data reveal that the majority of car-sharing users (58%) did not own a car before joining. This is bad news for the environmental performance of car sharing since those users increased their total amount of driving by definition, because they didn't have a car to drive in. A much smaller share of car-sharing users (25%) got rid of one or more owned vehicles after joining or didn't replace one that stopped working. Another 8% stated that they joined car sharing instead of buying a vehicle. The more important result is that 71% of respondents reported an increase in driving, while only 29% decreased their driving. However, the households that increased their driving did so by a fairly modest amount, while the ones that decreased their driving reported much larger reductions. As a result, the average overall change in driving was a reduction by 1,740 km per household per year. This number is conservative in that it does not account for the fact that the households that joined car sharing instead of buying a vehicle also reported that they would have driven more if they had bought a car. Since this alternative scenario never happened, it is counterfactual and thus fraught with extra uncertainty.

The answer to the second question, which is whether car sharing changes the fuel efficiency of the cars being driven is more straightforward. Yes, it does. The average fuel economy of the shared cars used by the survey respondents was 33 mile per gallon (mpg), 10 mpg higher than the average fuel economy of the owned cars used by the respondents. This means that, overall, switching from an owned to a shared car reduces greenhouse gas emissions, even if the driven distance doesn't change. Car sharing companies have, of course, an economic incentive to have fuel efficient cars in their fleet since they charge their members by the hour and include the fuel.

So far, we have only looked at changes in driving. Unfortunately, the Berkeley survey did not collect enough data to quantify the effect of changes in transportation modes. It is likely that previously carless house-holds reduced the use of alternative and public transportation modes. It is equally likely that households that reduced their number of owned cars increased it. The survey generated some data that suggest that the overall change might be fairly modest. When this is combined with the high effi-ciency of alternative and public transportation modes, the overall change in greenhouse gas emissions due to mode shifts can be expected to be relatively small. The Berkeley researchers go even further by arguing that trains and buses would run anyway, with or without the surveyed house-hold members, which makes the greenhouse gas emissions caused by their mode shifting minimal.

The final change we need to assess is the change in vehicle produc-tion caused by car sharing. The Berkeley researchers make no statement about this, but it appears that Zipcar used their numbers for the claim of each Zipcar taking 13 owned cars off the road. Zipcar counts all cars that car-sharing users shed after joining and all cars users say they would have bought as cars taken of the road. This method of counting ignores that many of the shed cars ended up on the used car market and are therefore still on the road and that some of the forgone cars would have been used cars, too. The predominant mechanism by which car sharing avoids vehi-cle production is by reducing the amount of driving, assuming that shared and owned cars have roughly the same lifetime in terms of total mile-age. This means that reduced vehicle production is a direct consequence of reduced driving. Using the driving reductions from the Berkeley survey suggests that the true number of avoided cars is somewhere between 0.5 and 1 car per shared car. That is nowhere near the 13 that Zipcar claims but still significant.

This is it. You just went through your first net green analysis. What have we learned? Car sharing appears to reduce overall greenhouse gas emissions. According to the Berkeley researchers, the average reduction is between 600 and 800 kg CO_2e per participating household and year. However, not every household reduces its emissions. In fact, the majority increase their emis-sions! Yet, these increases are more than outweighed by the much larger emission decreases of the other households. The main net green mecha-nism is an overall reduction in driving. A smaller, secondary mechanism is an increase in overall vehicle efficiency. Probably the most important insight is that car sharing is not net green in and of itself. It is net green only for those customers that drive less as a result of joining. That is simply impossible for the 58% of car-sharing users who didn't own a car before joining. Car sharing encourages those users to shift from more efficient alternative and public transportation modes to cars. This is a problem if a car-sharing company mostly targets those households as customers. To be a business of less, car sharing needs to be a catalyst for driving less, not more.

How is net green analysis different from life cycle assessment (LCA) as introduced in Chapter 3? The main difference is that net green assesses a change in the way we produce and consume while this type of LCA studies a given product life cycle, not a change in it. As discussed, this LCA approach has several downsides. One of them is that it is an eco-efficiency measure, quantifying environmental impact per unit product or service. An LCA comparing a pair of shoes from the case study in Chapter 5 before and after the technological breakthrough would simply show that the environmental impact per pair is now half of what it was before. The environmental rebound effects due to the cost savings would be completely unaccounted for, leading to an overestimate of the environmental benefits. In other words, a win-win assessed through traditional LCA would give you a completely wrong idea of its overall environmental impact. In a net green analysis, the economic cost savings would be a consequence with significant environmental implications.

This traditional type of LCA, which is called attributional, would also completely miss the main environmental benefits of car sharing, since it would compare the environmental impacts of driving a certain distance, say 100 km, in an owned car versus a shared car. It might pick up the different fuel efficiency between the owned and the shared car, but even that is not a given since the assessment might use the same car model for both scenarios in order to be 'fair'. There is an alternative type of LCA, called consequential, which addresses some of these shortcomings by studying the environmental implications of a change in a product system rather than the environmental impacts of a product system in a given state. Consequential LCA is a much more recent development than attributional LCA and has no universally agreed-upon methods yet. Whether the environmental consequences of cost savings would be included in consequential LCA or not is therefore unclear. However, net green analysis and consequential LCA are definitely cousins in that both study the environmental consequences of a change in a production and consumption systems.

A frequent criticism of consequential assessments is that some of the consequences of interest are subject to high uncertainty. What exactly do households spend additional cost savings on? What are the environmental consequences of saving money? What are the consequences of increasing the price of a product, the fuel efficiency of a car, or the recycling rate of a metal? I heard seasoned and senior LCA experts say that these high uncertainties make consequential assessments all but pointless and that it is thus better to stick with the well-established accounting-based attributional LCA. That view reminds me of the joke about a policeman finding a person on all fours in the dark of night under the lone streetlight of an empty parking lot. "What are you doing?" asks the policeman. "Looking for my car keys," says the clearly inebriated man. The policeman gets down on his knees and also starts looking. After ten minutes of futile searching, he says, "Are you sure you lost them here?" "No," says the man, "I lost them over there, but it's pitch-black over there." Or as Roland Clift likes to say: Some prefer being precisely wrong to being approximately right. Net green asks the important questions. If the answers are hard to come by, it just means we need to try harder. And the uncertainties themselves are important insights. If we're uncertain about the size of a rebound effect, maybe the lesson is to try to avoid it altogether. For example, maybe we should increase the cost of fuel as cars get more efficient so that the cost per distance stays the same.

The business of less is about reducing overall environmental impact. Does this imply reducing overall economic activity and output? The question whether environmental sustainability is reconcilable with continued economic growth goes back all the way to *Limits to Growth* and beyond. Probably the best-known of the modern proponents of a no-growth or steady-state economy is economist Herman Daly, who edited and published an influential collection of essays in 1973 called "Towards a Steady-State Economy."[6] More recently, Tim Jackson has rekindled the debate with his 2009 book *Prosperity without Growth*.[7] Needless to say that neither has any shortage of critics. The argument is ongoing and won't be officially settled anytime soon. That's true even within Germany's Green Party, which, by the way, has grown into a leading political force since its humble beginnings in 1980. Polls in 2019 suggested that the Green Party would receive around 25% of the national vote if there were elections.[8] At the state (Bundesland) level, the Green Party is now more often part of the government than part of the opposition. Even the German Green Party can't decide whether sustainable or green growth is a thing or a contradiction in terms.

Economic growth is virtually always measured as gross domestic product, or GDP, which is the value of all goods and services produced within a certain territory over a certain period. There are two degrees of separation between GDP and environmental impact. The first is the relationship between a physical good and the environmental impact caused by its production, use, and disposal. For example, the production of one ton of primary aluminum may generate 5 or 20 tons of CO_2e, depending on the GHG intensity of the used electricity.[9] The second is the relationship between the physical good and its economic value. For example, over the last five years, the price of a ton of aluminum varied between \$1,400 and \$2,400.[10] The aluminum example shows that the relationship between GDP and environmental impact, such as greenhouse gas emissions, is very variable, at least in principle. Increasing the share of low-carbon electricity in aluminum production will change that relationship, as will making aluminum more valuable/expensive. Yet, all we have to do is look at the figures in Chapter 4 to remind us that the whole project of decoupling, if there ever was one, has been a dismal failure so far. I would therefore argue that traditional economic growth is most certainly unsustainable. Any economic growth that could coincide with large or dramatic reductions in environmental impact would have to look radically different.

There are also growing calls to abandon GDP as the main measure for economic performance altogether. Even economists have started to join the call. Joseph Stiglitz recently threw his Nobel-memorial-prize-in-economic-sciences weight behind the growing discontent with GDP and pointed out that it does a very poor job at measuring what matters, like environmental degradation, economic inequality, democratic health, and social progress more broadly.[11] So, if GDP doesn't even measure what it is supposed to, there seems little reason to insist on a growing GDP in the first place. Luckily, we don't need to settle the debate about the compatibility of economic growth and environmental sustainability in order to use the net green concept, since it focuses squarely on environmental impact reduction.

Net green has been conceived as a tool to identify and assess opportunities to reduce or prevent pollution. As mentioned in Chapter 2, pollution prevention is seen as an attractive alternative to pollution control, which relies on so-called end-of-pipe technologies like baghouses, scrubbers, and wastewater treatment. Cleaning up pollution that has neither been prevented nor been controlled effectively is typically called remediation. Examples of remediation are cleaning up ocean waters and beaches after an oil spill or cleaning up soil after a chemical accident or chronic leak. There is no real reason why the net green concept can't be applied to pollution control or remediation activities. Having said that, the focus of this book is definitely pollution prevention, that is, reducing environmental impact by avoiding or reducing the generation of polluting wastes and emissions in the first place. In the case of anthropogenic climate change, which is the largest and most urgent environmental threat we are currently facing, it is not even clear if there will be any feasible control or remediation technologies in the near future. Remediation would mean removing CO_2, and possibly other greenhouse gases, from the atmosphere. Control would mean capturing CO_2, the most important greenhouse gas, from smokestacks and tailpipes. Once it is captured, we would need to use or deposit the carbon so that it doesn't escape back into the atmosphere. The combination of the two is typically called carbon capture and sequestration or CCS for short. While I am not entirely ruling out that there could be some breakthrough carbon remediation or capture and sequestration technology, I am not holding my breath. The laws of physics are just not in their favor. And I would certainly like to see a detailed net green analysis of any proposed technology. Even traditional life cycle assessment and thinking has revealed that these technologies typically entail large trade-offs and a high risk of unintended consequences. A recent publication suggested that we already have the best and most efficient carbon removal technology anyway; it's called a tree.[12] I haven't done one yet, but I think a net green analysis of tree planting would be fairly short and conclusive. Unfortunately, we are busy doing the opposite of reforestation. While I was writing this chapter, analysis of satellite data revealed that this year's deforestation in Brazil's Amazon rainforest was the worst since 2008.[13]

In the case of CO_2, pollution prevention is about finding ways to reduce our consumption of fossil fuels, so we can leave them in the ground. By leaving the fossil carbon where it is, we avoid the need to capture it from smokestacks and sequester it or remove it from the atmosphere. To me that seems a lot easier and thus a bit of a no-brainer. It turns out that there are just three general principles to prevent pollution, be it fossil CO_2 or anything else for that matter. To make them easy to remember I call them 'less', 'different', and 'again'. We will discuss them in detail in the following three chapters.

Notes

1   Gordon Gekko is a fictional character stemming from the 1987 film *Wall Street*. His name has become a symbol in pop culture for greed (at one point he states, "Greed, for lack of a better word, is good").

2   William Ripple et al., "World Scientists' Warning of a Climate Emergency," *BioScience* 70, no. 1 (2019): pp. 8–12, accessed July 21, 2020, https://academic.oup.com/bioscience/article/70/1/8/5610806.

3   Roland Geyer, "Parametric Assessment of Climate Change Impacts of Automotive Material Substitution," *Environmental Science and Technology* 42, no. 18 (2008): pp. 6973–6979, accessed January 13, 2021, https://doi.org/10.1021/es800314w.

4   "Carsharing," *Zipcar*, accessed July 21, 2020, www.zipcar.com/carsharing.

5   Elliot Martin and Susan Shaheen, "Greenhouse Gas Emission Impacts of Carsharing in North America," *IEEE Xplore: Transactions on Intelligent Transportation Systems* 12, no. 4 (2012): pp. 1074–1086, accessed January 13, 2021, www.researchgate.net/publication/224247227_Greenhouse_Gas_Emission_Impacts_of_Carsharing_in_North_America.

6   Herman E. Daly, *Toward a Steady-State Economy* (New York: W. H. Freeman Publisher, 1973).

7   Tim Jackson, *Prosperity Without Growth*, 1st ed. (London, UK: Routledge, 2009).

8   "Grüne legen in Umfragen weiter deutlich zu," *Spiegel*, last modified June 6, 2019, accessed January 13, 2021, www.spiegel.de/politik/deutschland/deutschlandtrend-gruene-legen-in-umfragen-weiter-deutlich-zu-a-1271270.html; Jochen Bittner, "The Greens Are Germany's Leading Political Party: Wait, What?," *The New York Times*, last modified June 19, 2019, accessed January 13, 2021, www.nytimes.com/2019/06/19/opinion/greens-party-germany.html.

9   "Life Cycle Inventory Data and Environmental Metrics for the Primary Aluminum Industry: 2015 Data," *International Aluminium Institute*, (June 2017), accessed January 13, 2021, www.world-aluminium.org/media/filer_public/2017/06/28/lca_report_2015_final.pdf.

10   "Aluminum," *Trading Economics*, accessed July 21, 2020, https://tradingeconomics.com/commodity/aluminum.

11   Joseph Stiglitz, "It's Time to Retire Metrics Like GDP: They Don't Measure Everything That Matters," *The Guardian*, last modified November 24, 2019, accessed July 21, 2020, www.theguardian.com/commentisfree/2019/nov/24/metrics-gdp-economic-performance-social-progress.

12   Jean-Francois Bastin et al., "The Global Tree Restoration Potential," *Science* 365, no. 6448 (July 2019): pp. 76–79, accessed January 13, 2021, https://science.sciencemag.org/content/365/6448/76.

13   "Tracking Amazon Deforestation from Above," *NASA Earth Observatory*, accessed July 21, 2020, https://earthobservatory.nasa.gov/images/145988/tracking-amazon-deforestation-from-above.

7

AGAIN

It was the early hours of July 19, 2017, but Carlyle Johnston was wide awake. Staring at the ceiling, the news he had read about the previous day just kept going round and round in his head. The implications were dire, and he knew he was in for a rough ride.

Fifteen years ago, in 2002, Carlyle had returned to his hometown Santa Barbara in Southern California to manage the curbside recycling programs for the county and many of its cities. He was passionate about his new job and also very good at it. Municipal solid waste recycling is driven by environmental goals like reducing the impacts from landfilling. Nonetheless, Carlyle took great pride in the fact that his curbside recycling program was a source of net revenue and thus reduced the cost of municipal solid waste management rather than adding to it.

In most U.S. municipalities, curbside recycling goes like this: In addition to the regular, typically brown, garbage bin, households are given a blue recycling bin and encouraged to throw all their recyclables into it. The contents of the blue bins go to a so-called material recovery facility (MRF,

DOI:10.4324/9781003163060-07

pronounced 'murf'), where they are sorted into material categories by a mix of people and technology. A significant portion of what is put in the blue bin is not recyclable and still ends up being landfilled or incinerated. In Santa Barbara, this non-recyclable fraction is 20% by mass, while the rest is about 40% paper, 20% glass, 15% cardboard, some percent metals and plastic each. In Santa Barbara and most communities in the United States, sorted recyclables are sold to brokers, who sell it on to the facilities that actually convert them into secondary materials, ready to be used again. The county pays a processing fee to the MRF but also receives most of the revenues from selling the sorted recyclables. The market values of sorted recyclables are notoriously volatile, but under Carlyle's management Santa Barbara County's recycling program had developed a track record of generating a substantial net revenue each year, much of it coming from paper and cardboard.

Like every June, Carlyle had generated a forecast for the upcoming fiscal year, and based on the projected revenues, 2017/2018 was going to be his best year ever. Then, on July 18, 2017, China's Ministry of Environmental Protection informed the World Trade Organization of its plans to ban the imports of many recyclables, unless they were shown to have only minimal contamination.[1] As always, over half of the county's recyclables were destined for China, and Carlyle instantly knew that those contamination limits were unattainable by his curbside recycling program, or any other program in the nation for that matter. As a result, the market values of recyclables were about to plummet, and instead of generating the largest revenues in his career, his recycling program was going to operate at a loss for the foreseeable future since the recyclables had nowhere else to go. Carlyle knew instinctively that recycling would never be the same.

Reuse and recycling is one of the three pollution prevention principles. I call it 'again' for short. Recycling means that we recover material from production or consumption waste and use it again. Reuse recovers not just material but also value added. You can reuse individual components from a product that has reached the end of its life, or you can reuse the entire product. Examples of the former would be to salvage functioning parts from cars that are about to be scrapped or reclaim building components from construction and demolition waste. Examples of the latter are buying secondhand clothes from a thrift store or the cell phone refurbishment discussed in Chapter 5. Component or product reuse goes by many other names, such as remanufacturing, refurbishment, or reconditioning. The idea is always the same: A product has reached the end of its use and is discarded by the owner. It is then collected and reprocessed by a third party or the original manufacturer, who sells the resulting secondary parts or products to its customers. Product repair is slightly different since the owner doesn't change. At the risk of splitting hairs, I would say that repair extends the current life of a product while reuse adds a second life. Reuse and recycling are probably as old as civilization itself, but it was the modern environmental movement that popularized them as strategies for environmental impact reduction. The cycling of material resources also lies at the heart of my academic field – industrial ecology. The very notion of the industrial ecosystem is motivated by the idea that we should learn from natural ecosystems how to 'close the loop'. More recently, reuse and recycling has been rebranded as the 'circular economy', in particular by the Ellen MacArthur Foundation and McKinsey.[2] These recent rebranding efforts successfully renewed the interest of policy makers in reuse and recycling, but this happened at the expense of reinventing the wheel and the missed chance of learning from past failures.

I say failure because for the moment we appear to be stuck in our current linear production paradigm. The word linear describes the fact that our supply chains are designed and optimized to extract virgin material resources from nature, turn those virgin materials into new products, and use those new products until we discard them as waste. As a result, most materials, wood, minerals, metals, glass, or plastics are used once and then end up in engineered landfills, open dumps, or the natural environment. In contrast to this linear, once-through production philosophy, reuse and recycling would create supply loops and thus reduce both natural resource extraction and waste disposal. Resource extraction and waste disposal are both associated with ecosystem disturbance and pollution, but avoiding these is not the only environmental benefit of reuse and recycling. It also turns out that the production processes involved in reuse and recycling typically have much lower environmental impacts than those involved in making new materials and products. The reasons for this are very intuitive. A metal ore, for example, is rock that contains the desired metal, which is typically oxidized or otherwise bonded together with other, mostly undesired, minerals. The metal content of ores varies widely from over 50% by mass to much less than 1%, depending on the type of metal and the type of ore. The concentration and purification processes required to produce pure primary metals from ore are therefore very energy- and resource-intensive and generate large amounts of wastes and emissions, many of them hazardous. Metal scrap, on the other hand, contains the pure metal, some alloying elements, and a typically small amount of contamination. Collecting and remelting scrap to produce recycled, also called secondary, metals therefore requires much less energy and generates much lower environmental impacts overall. On global average, for example, primary aluminum production is over 20 times as greenhouse gas intensive as aluminum recycling.[3] For steel this factor is not quite as large but still over four.[4] For other materials, such as plastic, paper, and glass, the differences in emissions between virgin production and recycling are not as dramatic but still very significant. In general, unless the scrap material is too contaminated, it takes much less effort to recycle scrap plastic, paper, and glass than to make those materials from fossil fuels, wood, sand, limestone, and soda ash.

The impact reduction potential of reuse is even larger than that of recycling. Again, the reasons for that are quite intuitive. Not only do reuse activities tend to have much lower environmental impacts than recycling activities, but they also recover entire components and products, not just their materials. Cell phone recycling, for example, recovers copper and precious metals by shredding the handsets and sending them to primary copper smelters.[5] Sometimes the steel and aluminum content is also recovered but no other materials are. The environmental impacts of cell phone collection, shipping, and recycling are lower than the impacts of producing equal amounts of primary metals from ore. However, this difference pales when compared to the difference between cell phone refurbishment and the production of an entire new handset. The environmental impacts of cell phone refurbishment are minimal and mostly come from transportation since the actual refurbishment mostly consists of labor. The environmental impact of producing a new cell phone, however, is large and mostly comes from making its electronic components. While the metals are worth recovering, they contribute a relatively small part to the total environmental impacts of cell phone production. In other words, the difference in environmental impact between cell phone recycling and equivalent primary metal production is modest, while the difference in environmental impact between cell phone refurbishment and equivalent new cell phone production is nothing short of spectacular.

The environmental case for reuse and recycling is thus compelling, yet, if anything, the 20th century is characterized by a move away from reuse and recycling and towards linear, once-through supply chains. Selling food, beverages, and most other household products in reusable containers used to be the norm until containers became so cheap and consumers so wealthy that they could afford to use containers once and then throw them away. Other single-use products, like disposable diapers, towels, napkins, cutlery, razors, and pens simply didn't exist at the beginning of the 20th century. Instead, there used to be an entire profession collecting unwanted items from households for reuse and recycling. These rag-and-bone men, as they were called in the UK, had all but vanished by the end of the century. Salvaging scrapped cars for spare parts used to be the norm, now it's hardly done anymore. And did you ever try to have a broken household appliance repaired? I rest my case.

So, what is stopping our economy from being more circular? The short answer is that the economics of reuse and recycling are currently too poor to successfully compete with linear, once-through supply chains, which take advantage of huge economies of scale and the ongoing replacement of labor with machines and automation. A closer look reveals that supply loops have to overcome three serious constraints, which makes them much more challenging than circular economy enthusiasts make it sound.[6] This should not come as a surprise. In conventional production, the upstream processes of suppliers produce output that is customized for the downstream processes of their customers, since the final good is the ultimate purpose of the entire supply chain. The inputs of supply loops, on the other hand, are products that are almost never designed for end-of-life value recovery. Supply loops also have to be organized in order to cope with the uncertain timing of the return of end-of-life products and the uncertain amount of their recoverable value. For these reasons, they are much more likely to be constrained than linear supply chains. There are three constraints, each of which can be caused by a mix of technical, operational, or economic challenges. In the end, though, it always comes down to economics since the greatest technology or operational approach is useless if it's too expensive.

The first supply loop constraint comes from the need to collect the waste products and materials from where they are generated and transport them to reprocessing facilities. Waste is generated by production and consumption activities. Examples of production or pre-consumer wastes are industrial and commercial packaging and production scrap from material processing like metal stamping, plastic molding, or fabric cutting. Post-consumer waste, also called municipal solid waste (MSW), is generated by households, schools, hospitals, and businesses. Pre-consumer waste is generated at fewer locations and frequently pre-sorted and baled. Post-consumer waste is generated at myriads of locations, frequently all mixed together, and typically suffers from contamination. All this makes collection of post-consumer waste for reuse and recycling costly and inefficient. By post-consumer waste, I don't just mean everything that goes into the garbage or recycling bin but all other waste like paint, old batteries, appliances, electronics, toys, sports equipment, furniture, mattresses, or clothes. None of these products are designed with end-of-life collection and value recovery in mind. I call a supply loop collection-constrained if it struggles to obtain end-of-life products and materials at the right time, in the right quantities, at the right cost, and with the right quality. Unfortunately, this is true more often than not.

Once production or consumption waste is collected, it has to be reprocessed into secondary materials, components, or products. Limited ability to do so constitutes the second constraint. There are many technical and economic reasons why reprocessing might be constrained. Some materials are more or less inherently unrecoverable. Examples are glass or carbon fiber reinforced plastics used to make things like boat hulls, surfboards, bicycle frames, and wind turbine blades. The plastics used to embed the fibers are called thermosets since they cannot be re-melted or reshaped once hardened. The best we can do with thermosets is to chop or grind them up at the end of their lives. There are efforts to at least recover the fibers, but I wouldn't hold my breath. As mentioned earlier, metals are highly recyclable as they can be re-melted, yet even metal recycling can suffer from reprocessing constraints. Copper contamination, for example, can limit steel recycling since copper is impossible to remove from molten steel and creates surface defects. Other materials, like paper and cardboard, can only be recycled a limited number of times. Each time paper fibers are re-pulped, their length is reduced until they are too short to be of much use. For some materials, recycling is technically feasible but simply not cost competitive. The best example for this is probably plastic. Most plastics we use are so-called thermoplastics and, in contrast to the thermosets mentioned earlier, can be re-melted and reshaped. This makes them recyclable in principle but frequently not in practice. In order to obtain valuable recycled plastic with good technical properties, collected plastic waste has to be separated by polymer type and cleaned in order to remove all other materials and contaminants. The resulting clean single-polymer flakes can then be re-melted and re-extruded into recycled, or secondary, plastic pellets. Unfortunately, the cost of doing all this tends to be higher than the cost of producing virgin, or primary, plastic pellets. A 2020 U.S. documentary by NPR and PBS revealed that even the plastic industry had serious doubts that recycling would ever be viable, which did not stop them from promoting it in order to fend off environmental legislation.[7]

Product or component reuse has its own set of reprocessing challenges. One of them is the frequent need to disassemble the collected end-of-life product in order to extract the reusable components or to remanufacture or refurbish the product. Today's products are not designed for disassembly, which makes it either very labor-intensive or simply impossible without damage. The actual remanufacturing or reconditioning processes also tend to be very labor-intensive and thus too costly to support viable business models.

The third constraint is created by the trivial, but important, fact that there needs to be sufficient market demand for the outputs of supply loops. Most potential customers value secondary materials, components, and products less than their primary counterparts. This can be because secondary output does have reduced quality or technical specifications or because customers intrinsically value newness even if the secondary output is technically equivalent.

Together, the three supply loop constraints generate the following dilemma: The cost of secondary materials, components, and products tends to be higher than their value. Increasing the value, say through better collection, separation, or reprocessing, also increases the cost. If the cost increase exceeds the increase in value, there's no point in doing so. There are success stories, where the cost of collection and reprocessing is consistently lower than the value of the secondary output. Examples include recycling steel and aluminum from end-of-life construction, infrastructure, machinery, and transportation equipment, such as cars, trucks, trains, airplanes, and ships. Other examples include recycling certain packaging made from cardboard, glass, steel, aluminum, and the polymers #1 and #2 (polyethylene terephthalate, PET, and high-density polyethylene, HDPE). Yet, even PET bottles, the "superstar of plastic recycling" as one industry expert calls them, has a U.S. recycling rate of only 28%, meaning that over 2 out of 3 PET bottles still end up as discarded waste.[8]

The collection rate would be even lower if it wasn't for the ten U.S. States that have so-called bottle bills, which dramatically increase collection rates by adding a redeemable deposit to the beverage sales price.[9] Charging a redeemable deposit or a non-redeemable recycling fee is one way to address supply loop constraints. Another is to set and require specific supply loop targets, such as collection rates, recycling rates, or recycled content in new products. The umbrella term for all these policy approaches is 'extended producer responsibility' or EPR for short. Alternative names for EPR are product stewardship or product take-back legislation. The main purpose of EPR legislation is to establish viable supply loops by alleviating their constraints. One of the first EPR legislations was Germany's original Packaging Ordinance (VerpackV) from 1991. Over the last twenty years, the European Union has passed a number of EPR directives, which recently culminated in the adoption of a Circular Economy Action Plan. In the United States, EPR legislation is currently only pursued at the state level.

In Chapter 5, I suggested that we should not require that opportunities for environmental impact reduction also reduce cost but instead regard impact reduction as added value. In the case of reuse and recycling, this means that secondary output should be more, not less, valuable than their primary counterparts. Ideally, we, the customers, would willingly pay a price premium for recycled content and the environmental impact reduction it entails. If we cannot be persuaded to do so, then EPR and other policies are needed to bridge the current viability gap of supply loops. In other words, at this point we may have to accept that supply loops have great environmental potential but are not the incredible market opportunities that some naïve supporters suggest and require deft and robust policy interventions instead.

Now, unfortunately, overcoming the three supply loop constraints is not enough to make sure that reuse and recycling reduce environmental impacts. This is due to the following critically important insight: The only environmental purpose of reuse and recycling is to reduce the production and consumption of primary materials, components, and products. This simple fact is wildly underappreciated, even among circular economy experts. Typically, it is assumed that reuse and recycling achieved their environmental objectives once the secondary resource has found its way back into the economy, i.e. the loop has been closed. Yet making a particular reuse or recycling activity operationally, technically, and economically viable is not enough to guarantee its environmental success. Here's why: The collection and reprocessing activities involved in supply loops have their own environmental impacts, like emissions from transportation and recycling processes. On its own, diverting waste from landfill or incineration and reprocessing it into secondary products, parts, or materials therefore actually increases total environmental impacts. Net environmental benefits are created when the avoided environmental impacts from reduced primary production and waste disposal are larger than the incurred environmental impacts from collection and reprocessing.

Let's unpack the earlier statement with the help of an example. Collecting aluminum scrap and turning it into a secondary aluminum ingot generates roughly 0.5 kg of CO_2e per kg of ingot. The greenhouse gas (GHG) intensity of a North American primary aluminum ingot is right around 9 kg CO_2e per kg. Landfilling a kg of aluminum scrap, on the other hand, generates less than 50 grams of CO_2e.[10] This means that the GHG savings potential of aluminum recycling is enormous and that virtually all of it comes from avoiding primary aluminum production, not avoiding landfill. I say potential because first aluminum recycling needs to reduce primary aluminum production. "What else would it do?" you may ask, and you wouldn't be alone. I have been getting this question from quite a few colleagues. A renowned LCA expert was so certain that all that material recycling can do is to reduce primary material production that he started to shout at me and questioned my intelligence. Yet there is no conservation law in physics that demands that recycling must reduce primary material production. The interaction between recycled and primary material is market-mediated and thus firmly in the realm of economics.[11] So, how do we know that recycled material doesn't compete with all kinds of materials on the market? How do we know that recycled material is not consumed in addition to rather than instead of all the other materials? The short answer is that we don't. In fact, basic microeconomic theory tells us that adding supply to a market is almost guaranteed to grow demand, at least somewhat. This is particularly true if the new additional supply is offered at a lower price, the very thing that is typically demanded of recycled material, even if it is technically equivalent.

What is the empirical evidence that recycling reduces primary materials production? Figure 1.4 in Chapter 1 shows that production of our main structural materials keeps increasing across the board. Global annual primary aluminum production increased more than threefold since the Earth Summit less than thirty years ago. Could it be that it would have grown even more if we hadn't recycled aluminum scrap? This question uses so-called counterfactual logic along the lines of "what would have happened if we hadn't done x?" which makes it extremely hard to answer. As part of Trevor Zink's PhD research, he and I teamed up with economist and econometrician Dick Startz to answer that question for aluminum in North America by trying to determine own- and cross-price elasticities of primary and secondary aluminum supply and demand.[12] Despite our best econometric efforts based on the best available data, the uncertainties in our results were enormous. We have since learned that price elasticities are notoriously difficult to estimate. The only thing we can say for sure is that it is extremely unlikely that aluminum recycling displaced primary aluminum production one to one. In other words, aluminum recycling almost certainly increased total aluminum use; we just don't know by how much. If this reminds you of the rebound effect discussed in Chapter 4, you're not alone. Due to the similarity, Trevor and I call the effect of recycling increasing total material consumption 'circular economy rebound'.[13]

The so-called waste-management hierarchy (reduce, reuse, recycle) is predicated on the assumption that reusing a product or component or recycling a certain amount of material avoids the production of an equivalent amount of new product, component, or material. It is entirely possible that recycling a certain product is the environmentally preferable thing to do if reusing it doesn't really avoid any new products from being made.

Sometimes I hear that, even without avoiding primary production, recycling at least diverts waste from landfill or incineration. Unfortunately, that is incorrect. Disposal is only avoided if primary production is avoided.[14] Otherwise, recycling only delays disposal, since all material eventually requires disposal. In the long run, the total amount of material disposal equals the total amount of primary material production. Or as Trevor likes to say, "the only material that needn't be disposed of is the one we never made."

It is correct, though, that aluminum recycling reduces the average carbon intensity of aluminum production, even if it does not displace a single ton of primary aluminum. But that's beside the point since we need to reduce total GHG emissions, not just reduce the GHG intensity of an ever-growing output. You may want to re-read Chapter 4 if you're not convinced.

The renewed interest in reuse and recycling is generating an ever-growing wave of circular economy indicators, which are all meant to measure our progress towards circularity. There is a plethora of possible indicators, which quickly becomes overwhelming: Collection rates, recycling rates, recycling yields, recycled input, recycled output, recycled content, average carbon intensities, and that's just for recycling. Now we can do the same again for component and product reuse. You can also find impassioned discussions of upcycling versus downcycling and closed-loop versus open-loop recycling. Each of these indicators and concepts tells us something about our efforts to close our material and product loops, but each one of them is at risk of missing the mark since the only point of reuse and recycling is to reduce primary production. The ultimate circular economy indicator is therefore annual primary production. As long as annual primary production increases, reuse and recycling are failing as pollution prevention strategies. It is hard to overstate the importance of this insight. For example, as long as virgin plastic production continues to grow 4% year over year over year, nothing we do to fix plastic recycling will increase the environmental sustainability of plastic.[15] The only environmental role of plastic recycling is to bend the curve of annual primary plastic production downwards or that of any other material it displaces.

In summary, reuse and recycling can be powerful net green strategies IF they are used to reduce our reliance on primary products and materials. The guiding principle should be to maximize the reduction in total environmental impact, that is, the difference between incurred impacts from collection and reprocessing and avoided impacts from displaced primary production and waste disposal.[16] A business active in the circular economy therefore needs to assess its impact on primary production in order to gauge its environmental performance. In other words, it is not enough to just create a circular economy. Instead, what matters is to what extent the circular economy does away with our current linear economy.

Notes

1   Tom Miles and Louise Ireland, "China Notifies WTO of Ban on Plastic, Paper, Textile Waste Imports," *Reuters*, last modified July 18, 2017, accessed July 21, 2020, www.reuters.com/article/china-environment/china-notifies-wto-of-ban-on-plastic-paper-textile-waste-imports-idUSL5N1K94IS.

2 "Towards the Circular Economy," *Ellen Macarthur Foundation*, (2013), accessed July 21, 2020, www.ellenmacarthurfoundation.org/assets/downloads/publications/Ellen-MacArthur-Foundation-Towards-the-Circular-Economy-vol.1.pdf.

3 "UCSB Energy & GHG Model, Version 5.0," *World Auto Steel*, accessed January 13, 2021, www.worldautosteel.org/life-cycle-thinking/ucsb-energy-ghg-model/.

4 "UCSB Energy & GHG Model, Version 5.0," *World Auto Steel*, accessed January 13, 2021, www.worldautosteel.org/life-cycle-thinking/ucsb-energy-ghg-model/.

5 Roland Geyer and Vered Blass, "The Economics of Cell Phone Reuse and Recycling," *Journal of Advanced Manufacturing Technology* 47, nos. 5–8 (September 2009): pp. 515–525, accessed January 13, 2021, https://link.springer.com/article/10.1007/s00170-009-2228-z.

6 Roland Geyer and Tim Jackson, "Supply Loops and Their Constraints: The Industrial Ecology of Recycling and Reuse," *California Management Review* 40, no. 2 (January 2004): pp. 55–73, accessed January 13, 2021, https://doi.org/10.2307%2F41166210.

7 Plastic Wars, "Season 20: Episode 14," *PBS Frontline video*, 54 minutes, March 31, 2020, www.pbs.org/wgbh/frontline/film/plastic-wars/.

8 "2019 PET Recycling Report," *National Association for PET Container Resources*, (December 2020), accessed January 6, 2021, https://napcor.com/news/4970-2/; Steve Toloken, "My Take on Frontline's Plastic Wars," *Plastic News*, last modified April 23, 2020, accessed January 13, 2021, www.plasticsnews.com/viewpoint/my-take-frontlines-plastic-wars.

9 These 10 states are: California, Connecticut, Hawaii, Iowa, Maine, Massachusetts, Michigan, New York, Oregon, and Vermont.

10 Joseph Palazzo and Roland Geyer, "Consequential Life Cycle Assessment of Automotive Material Substitution: Replacing Steel with Aluminum in North American Vehicle Production," *Environmental Impact Assessment Review* 75 (2019): pp. 47–58, accessed January 13, 2021, https://doi.org/10.1016/j.eiar.2018.12.001.

11 Trevor Zink, Roland Geyer, and Richard Startz, "A Market-Based Framework for Quantifying Displaced Production from Recycling or Reuse," *Journal of Industrial Ecology* 20, no. 4 (July 2015): pp. 719–729, accessed January 13, 2021, https://doi.org/10.1111/jiec.12317.

12 Trevor Zink, Roland Geyer, and Richard Startz, "Toward Estimating Displaced Production from Recycling: A Case Study of U.S. Aluminum," *Journal of Industrial Ecology* 22, no. 2 (March 2017): pp. 314–326, accessed January 13, 2021, https://doi.org/10.1111/jiec.12557.

13 Trevor Zink and Roland Geyer, "Circular Economy Rebound," *Journal of Industrial Ecology* 21, no. 3 (February 2017): pp. 593–602, accessed January 13, 2021, https://doi.org/10.1111/jiec.12545.

14 Trevor Zink and Roland Geyer, "Recycling and the Myth of Landfill Diversion," *Journal of Industrial Ecology* 23, no. 3 (August 2018): pp. 541–548, accessed January 13, 2021, https://doi.org/10.1111/jiec.12808.

15 Roland Geyer, Jenna R. Jambeck, and Kara Lavender Law, "Production, Use, and Fate of All Plastics Ever Made," *Science Advances* 3, no. 7 (2017): e1700782, accessed July 21, 2020, https://advances.sciencemag.org/content/3/7/e1700782.

16 Roland Geyer et al., "Common Misconceptions About Recycling," *Journal of Industrial Ecology* 20, no. 5 (October 2015): pp. 1010–1017, accessed January 13, 2021, https://doi.org/10.1111/jiec.12355.

8

DIFFERENT

In fall 2009, I was asked by an organic dairy to assist them with a packaging project. The company wanted to change the material of their yogurt cups, which was polystyrene (also known as PS or #6 plastic), to something more environmentally friendly. The food industry had started to move away from PS as packaging material, at least partially driven by the fact that it had the word styrene in its name. Styrene, the monomer that the polymer PS is made of, is a known toxicant and carcinogen. The dairy was considering a switch to polylactide (also known as polylactic acid or PLA), which is made from fermented plant starch and therefore a so-called bio-based polymer. The yogurt company was in conversation with NatureWorks, the world's largest polylactide producer, which makes PLA out of corn starch and sells it under the brand name Ingeo. NatureWorks started as a joint venture between agricultural giant Cargill and the equally large Dow Chemical Company.

Originally, PLA was marketed as a polymer that is made from renewable resources and also biodegradable, as opposed to traditional polymers,

DOI:10.4324/9781003163060-08

like PS, which are all made from fossil fuels and don't biodegrade. In other words, PLA was advertised as a greener alternative to conventional plastic because it was both bio-based and biodegradable. The use of a food or feed crop like corn to make plastic received some criticism, but the biodegradability claim proved to be the bigger problem. PLA requires industrial composting facilities. A backyard compost heap or bin is no good since PLA doesn't really degrade under those circumstances. The vast majority of households have no access to industrial composting. Even industrial composters aren't fond of items made from PLA since they take too long to biodegrade and frequently arrive with a significant amount of contamination, such as other non-biodegradable plastics.

By the time the dairy considered the switch from PS to PLA, NatureWorks was promoting its polymer mostly as a climate-change-mitigating low-carbon material, due to the fact that the carbon it is made of is sequestered from the atmosphere during the growth of the corn. My task was to review and compare the existing environmental assessments of PLA and PS. The first thing I noticed was that PLA was low-carbon only if it wasn't composted at the end of its use, since composting would convert all the sequestered carbon into CO_2 again and release it back into the atmosphere. This means that PLA can be biodegradable or low-carbon, but it can't be both. NatureWorks even commissioned studies to show that Ingeo would not biodegrade in landfill.

More importantly, though, it turned out that PLA performed worse than PS when it came to the environmental issues of acidification and eutrophication. Acidification is an excess of hydrogen ions in the environment, while eutrophication is an excess of nutrients on land or in waterbodies. Both can severely disrupt ecosystems. PLA's large eutrophication impact is unsurprising, since fertilizer run-off from agriculture is a major source of excess nutrients. In a nutshell, I found that switching from PS to PLA would reduce GHG emissions, given that the PLA was not composted, but increase eutrophication and acidification impacts. Given that PLA also diverts agricultural land from food to material production, the environmental case for the switch from PS to PLA was anything but clear-cut.

Material, product, or technology substitution is the second of the three pollution prevention principles. I call it 'different' for short. The basic idea is to replace an environmentally problematic substance, material, product, or technology with something else that can provide the same service without causing the environmental problem. I would argue that this approach is our current go-to strategy when dealing with environmental issues. Changing packaging materials, like in our yogurt cup case study, is a pertinent example. Attempts to make packaging more sustainable frequently focus on finding a 'green' packaging material. This is currently happening with a renewed sense of urgency. Since 2009, when the dairy wished to move away from polystyrene, all plastics have come under renewed environmental fire. In fact, public opinion has recently turned so swiftly that Stephen Buranyi wrote a so-called "The long read" article for The Guardian titled "The plastic backlash: what's behind our sudden rage – and will it make a difference?"[1] This backlash is not entirely surprising since plastic waste is increasingly visible in the natural environment, in particular in the world's oceans and on their shorelines. Many people seem to get particularly upset by images of marine life and seabirds entangled in or otherwise harmed by plastic debris. As a result, governments all over the world are implementing or considering bans on single-use plastic items that are commonly found on beaches or in the oceans, such as bags, plates, cutlery, and straws. Banning a particular product typically means that something else is going to be used in its stead. The big environmental question of such a ban is whether the alternatives that will be used instead of the banned items are a real environmental improvement, just as bad, or even worse. In other words, material, product, or technology substitutions require a net green analysis, as introduced in Chapter 6. We need to assess all relevant environmental consequences of the substitution. The obvious positive consequence of a product ban is that it avoids production, use, and disposal of said product. The less visible negative consequences come from the production, use, and disposal of the alternatives. There are two types of environmental trade-offs that we need to look out for when assessing a material, product, or technology substitution.

The first one is a trade-off across environmental concerns. This is what the dairy faced, since switching from PS to PLA was expected to reduce GHG emissions but increase ecosystem damage due to acidification and eutrophication. Unfortunately, the dairy case study is not an exception. Substitution strategies frequently suffer from this type of trade-off. Here is an early example that goes back almost one hundred years: The commercial use of compressor refrigerators expanded in the late 19th and early 20th century but relied on toxic and highly flammable refrigerants, such as ammonia, sulfur dioxide, and methyl chloride. It was not uncommon for commercial refrigerators to catch fire, explode, or leak toxic gases. The chlorofluorocarbons (CFCs) discussed in Chapter 2 not only made excellent refrigerants but were also nontoxic and nonflammable. Thomas Midgley famously demonstrated this in 1930 at a meeting of the American Chemical Society when he inhaled CFC-12 (CCl_2F_2) and blew out a candle with it. Using CFCs instead of the old refrigerants dramatically increased human health and safety and thus facilitated the expansion of refrigerators into the residential market. Unfortunately, as you already know, CFCs also deplete the ozone layer in the stratosphere. In addition, CFCs also have some of the highest global warming potentials (GWPs) of all greenhouse gases. Hydrofluorocarbons (HFCs), which replaced CFCs in the wake of the Montreal Protocol, don't contain the ozone-destroying element chlorine but still have extremely high GWPs. So, the search for a truly green refrigerant continues. As mentioned in Chapter 2, one proposal is to use propane and isobutene, which are, of course, flammable.

Here is another more recent example: When leaded gasoline was finally banned, methyl tertiary butyl ether (MTBE or $C_5H_{12}O$) quickly became a popular replacement. MTBE is an antiknock and octane booster, like TEL, but also an oxygenate, which means that its oxygen content helps gasoline to combust more completely and thus reduces harmful emissions. However, MTBE not only has an extremely foul odor and taste but is also highly water soluble. As a result, leaks or spills of MTBE-containing gasoline were causing persistent groundwater contamination issues, which eventually led to MTBE bans across the United States.

Trade-offs across environmental issues are so common in material, product, or technology substitutions that comparative environmental evaluation methods, such as life cycle assessment (LCA), are explicitly designed to catch and quantify them. The diaper controversy discussed in Chapter 3 was predicated on such a trade-off. The LCA commissioned by P&G in 1990 found that its single-use diaper required seven times the amount of raw materials and generated seven times more solid waste than reusable diapers, which in turn consumed three times the amount of energy and six times the amount of water, mostly due to diaper laundering.[2] This is a deeply unsatisfactory but fairly intuitive result. The reusable diaper is (as the name readily gives away) used over and over and therefore much less material-intensive than single-use diapers. However, it is being washed after every use (or so I hope), which requires water, detergent, and electricity. This makes the reusable diaper more water- and energy-intensive. This specific trade-off generally happens when a single-use item is compared to a reusable one that requires washing in between uses. Pertinent examples are environmental comparisons between single-use and multi-use beverage containers or between single-use and reusable coffee cups. The trade-off is unavoidable unless producing the single-use item is more water- and energy-intensive than washing and drying the reusable one.

Trade-offs across environmental concerns should generally be expected when equivalent products are made from distinct materials, especially when the two materials are fundamentally different. An absolute classic is the choice between single-use items made from paper or plastic. I can feel all you environmentally minded readers tense up just reading the words 'paper or plastic'. If it's any consolation, the same happens to environmental professionals. Over the decades, the environmental assessments of the paper versus plastic question have become more sophisticated, but the trade-offs have not gone away; they just shifted shape. Let's use paper and expanded polystyrene (EPS) foam cups as example. In the days before life cycle thinking, the comparison would be based solely on environmental product attributes. Is the product made from renewable or non-renewable resources? Is it biodegradable? Is it recyclable? The results are typically as confusing as they are meaningless. You could claim that the paper cup is more environmentally friendly because it is made from renewable resources and also biodegrades in many environments. Or you could say that the paper cup is worse because it is responsible for forest clear-cutting and causes methane and other emissions when decomposing anaerobically in landfills. A 1991 publication in *Science* tried to bring a more rigorous LCA perspective to the debate but arguably only made things worse.[3] It didn't help that the analysis used old paper mill data and overall seemed biased in favor of the plastic foam cup, which caused a fierce response from the paper industry. It also didn't help that LCA theory and practice had not been harmonized yet (see Chapter 3). A 2007 LCA from a reputable Dutch research organization had the advantage of a more mature LCA methodology backed up by ISO standards and came to the following conclusion: In five out of ten categories, the paper cup had lower environmental impacts. In the other five, it was the plastic cup.[4]

Trade-offs between a set of environmental concerns can also turn into an overall draw when switching to a different set of impact categories. A 2005 LCA commissioned by UK's Environment Agency revisited the diaper controversy but used ISO-approved methods and modern environmental impact indicators like global warming, acidification, and eutrophication. It came to the following conclusion: "There was no significant difference between any of the environmental impacts – that is, overall no system clearly had a better or worse environmental performance, although the life cycle stages that are the main source for these impacts are different for each system."[5]

The Environment Agency's summary is the perfect segue into the second type of environmental trade-off, which is across life cycle stages. Even if we are only concerned with a single environmental issue, say climate change, and don't care about anything else, we still have to be on the lookout for trade-offs within the studied product life cycles and even beyond. An excellent example is the GHG controversy around corn-based ethanol. The use of ethanol and other biofuels in internal combustion engines goes all the way back to the invention of the automobile itself. However, after the Second World War, Brazil was the only country with a substantial bioethanol program until the United States created the Renewable Fuel Standard (RFS) in 2005. To count towards the standard, each renewable fuel needs to have lower GHG emissions than the fuel it replaces. A flurry of life cycle GHG assessments of corn-based ethanol ensued, with widely contradicting results. The one thing everyone agreed on is that corn-based ethanol is certainly not GHG neutral. It's true that the CO_2 emissions from combusting bioethanol are equal to the amount of CO_2 that was sequestered during biomass growth, but plenty of additional GHGs are emitted during fertilizer and pesticide production, corn farming, and ethanol refining. So, substituting gasoline with ethanol shifts GHG emissions from fuel combustion to fuel production. But does it result in a net reduction or a net increase? In other words, is corn-based ethanol net green?

A meta-analysis of existing studies, published in Science in 2006, concluded that corn-based ethanol offers moderate (13%) GHG emission reductions relative to gasoline.[6] Unfortunately, this was not the end of the controversy. In 2008, two seminal papers were published in the same issue of Science, both arguing that GHG emissions from biofuels were underestimated. The first one pointed out that converting natural habitat to agricultural land for fuel crop production generates large amounts of GHG emissions, which need to be added to the GHG balance of biofuels. The authors found that biofuels require 17–420 years to just repay this 'carbon debt'.[7] The second paper argued that using existing farmland for fuel crops does not avoid the issue.[8] For example, diverting existing corn production from feed to fuel generates a feed shortfall, which needs to be met otherwise. This results in land conversions elsewhere, an effect now known as 'indirect land use change' or iLUC. The resulting GHG emissions are thus caused by increasing production of corn-based ethanol and need to be added to its GHG balance. In fact, California's Low Carbon Fuel Standard does just that. Despite what special interest groups might tell you, the emerging scientific consensus is that, as a climate change mitigation strategy, corn-based ethanol is somewhere between useless and terrible.

We don't have to go far to show that trade-offs across life cycle stages are not uncommon in material, product, or technology substitutions. An alternative approach to reduce GHG emissions from cars is to reduce their mass using so-called light-weight materials. The most discussed and practiced substitution is to replace steel with fiber-reinforced polymers or aluminum. One high-profile example is Ford's decision to switch the entire body structure of its 2015 F150 pickup truck, America's bestselling vehicle, from steel to aluminum. Ford states that, relative to the 2014 model, this enabled a vehicle mass reduction of 700 pounds (318 kg), which in turn increased the pickup's fuel economy by 20%.[9] Unfortunately, a vehicle body structure can't be made from recycled aluminum and thus requires primary aluminum, at least for now. I say unfortunately because you've learned in Chapter 7 that primary aluminum production is very GHG intensive – 20 times as much as recycled aluminum and still serval times as much as primary steel. As a result, the material substitution in the Ford 150 decreased the GHG emissions of driving the vehicle but increased the GHG emissions of making it. So, again the question is: What are the overall GHG consequences of the material substitution. Or was Ford's shift to aluminum net green?

As you would expect, the aluminum industry assures us that it was, while the steel industry insists that it was not. Unsurprisingly, the two industries argue over the amount of mass savings that the use of aluminum instead of steel can achieve and also the relationship between vehicle mass reduction and fuel consumption. It turns out, however, that the largest controversy is over the GHG consequences of using recycled steel or aluminum in vehicle production and the GHG consequences of recycling the vehicle at the end of its life.[10] I will spare you the esoteric details of this debate. Even my students struggle to get their heads around them. It took me a good long while, too. I recently noticed with some alarm that I have been studying the GHG implications of using light-weight materials to reduce vehicle mass for fifteen years now. My main lesson? If you want to be sure that vehicle mass reduction is net green, don't worry about the materials, just make the car smaller.

Before you give up on 'different' as a net green strategy, there are material, product, and technology substitutions that are not marred by environmental trade-offs. Ethanol, for example, is now used in the United States and elsewhere as a replacement for MTBE as both antiknock and oxygenate. As far as I can tell, this has been a net green move across the board. If anything, it is tragic that this move did not happen sooner, say in the early 1920s, when Midgley, Kettering, and others at General Motors and DuPont could have chosen ethanol over tetraethyl lead as antiknock (see Chapter 2). That would have saved the world seventy years of lead pollution.

Without doubt the most important technology substitution that we all should support and demand is the replacement of fossil-based electricity generation with renewable electricity such as wind and solar power. We should do this as if our future depends on it because it does. The primary driver of this substitution is, of course, to mitigate climate change by reducing the GHG emissions from electricity generation. There is no controversy whatsoever that the life cycle GHG emissions per kilowatt hour (g CO_2e/kWh) from renewable generation technologies are much, much lower than those from fossil-based power plants. There are literally hundreds of LCAs for electricity generation and, unsurprisingly, their results do vary. The National Renewable Energy Laboratory (NREL) of the U.S. Department of Energy went through the trouble of reviewing and harmonizing many of them.[11] The highest reported GHG intensities they found for wind, hydro, and solar photovoltaic (PV) electricity were 80, 165, and 220 g CO_2e/kWh, respectively. The lowest reported GHG intensities for natural gas and coal power plants were 310 and 650 g CO_2e/kWh, respectively. However, the medians for all reviewed LCAs were (all in g CO_2e/kWh) 1,000 for coal, 470 for natural gas, 55 for solar PV, 12 for wind, and 7 for hydro. If you need to store the renewable electricity before you can use it, you can add battery storage for roughly another 50 g CO_2e/kWh.[12]

Wind and solar power have also been shown to have much lower impacts across a wide range of other environmental concerns. Furthermore, they don't require more land than fossil-based power generation, as is sometimes claimed.[13] Reservoir-based hydropower needs to make sure that methane emissions from decaying biomass are small and also tends to be more controversial when it comes to land use impacts. Now that wind power and utility-scale solar are also the cheapest ways to generate electricity, substituting fossil power plants with wind and solar technologies is simply a no-brainer. The case for wind and solar power is now so overwhelming that opponents need to resort to ever more outlandish claims. If you're really worried about birds being killed, for example, you should go talk to your cat instead of blaming wind turbines. And you should do something about climate change.

In my second example, I am going to come out strongly in favor of electro-mobility in general, and electric vehicles (EVs) in particular, even though I readily admit that EVs are a bit more controversial than wind and solar power. I would argue that this is mostly due to the fact that EVs and their environmental assessments are both newer and less mature than wind and solar technologies and their assessments. I can already see a scientific consensus forming about the many environmental advantages of EVs relative to our current internal combustion vehicles (ICVs) and predict that any remaining controversies will be gone soon. In the early 1990s, California supported EVs as a way to reduce air pollution in conurbations like Greater Los Angeles. Today, they are mostly championed as a way to reduce GHG emissions from the transportation sector. As we just discussed, the electricity that EVs run on has its own GHG footprint, and it is also true that EV production emits more GHGs than making a comparable ICV. However, every serious recent study came to the conclusion that, even with the GHG intensities of current electricity grids, EVs already have lower life cycle GHG emissions than comparable ICVs.[14] The higher production emissions of EVs are caused by the battery required for onboard electricity storage. Around 50% of the GHG emissions from battery production are actually from the electricity utilized in the manufacturing process.[15] This means that a declining GHG intensity of electricity not only reduces the use phase emissions of EVs but also their production emissions. I don't want to trivialize the environmental impacts from some materials required for popular battery chemistries, such as lithium and cobalt, but I do believe that they are perfectly manageable if we put our mind to it. To begin with, we need to make sure to recover these metals from retired batteries. Recycling the batteries would also mitigate some of the other environmental impacts of battery production, such as eutrophication. Unless we decide to abandon cars altogether, EVs are our best environmental bet. We already know how to generate and distribute electricity, electric powertrains are extremely efficient, and there are many ancillary benefits, like the fact that electric powertrains require zero engine oil and very little maintenance and repair.

My final example for a clearly net green substitution is changing the sources of protein in our diet. When it comes to GHG emissions, or environmental impacts more broadly, there is a well-researched and well-documented hierarchy of protein sources. GHG emissions (all in kg CO_2e/50g protein) range from 0.2 for pulses to 12.2 for beef. In between are 0.6 for tuna, 2.7 for poultry and pork, and 3.3 for tilapia.[16] So, replacing beef with any old protein source is more or less guaranteed to be net green. The reason for this is simply that raising cattle is a uniquely inefficient and impactful way to produce protein. So, just shifting from beef to poultry, pork, or fish leads to significant reductions in GHGs and other environmental impacts. However, there is no doubt that the largest impact reductions are achieved if beef or any other meat-based protein is substituted with plant-based protein. This insight is very important, since agriculture and food production are responsible for a quarter of all our GHG emissions and a major source of many other environmental impacts through its use of fertile land and reliance on monocultures, irrigation, and agrochemicals. The insight is also somewhat trivial. Of course, we can dramatically reduce environmental impacts if we eat plants instead of feeding the plants to animals and then eat the animals. It takes about ten pounds of feed to produce one pound of beef.[17]

Unfortunately, the world has been moving in the opposite direction. Over the decades, the animal share of protein consumption has been increasing, as has total protein consumption. In many developed economies, daily protein intake is now over 100 grams per person, even though the recommended amount is 50 grams.[18] It's not all bad news, though. One of my PhD students recently found that the GHG footprint of the U.S. diet has been decreasing significantly since 2002, driven by a reduction in beef consumption.[19]

So, where does this all leave us? 'Different' can be a powerful pollution prevention strategy, but it carries a significant risk of environmental trade-offs, which could lead to regrettable substitutions. This means that any considered material, product, or technology substitution needs to be carefully assessed using the net green analysis framework. The environmental trade-off can be across environmental issues or across life cycle stages. It could even take place outside of the actual product life cycles, as illustrated by the phenomenon of indirect land use change (iLUC). Some environmental trade-offs may be acceptable, but, ideally, we should look for ways to reduce environmental impact across the board. A persistent, unacceptable environmental trade-off may mean that we need to look for other pollution prevention strategies. If 'different' doesn't work, you could try 'less', the strategy discussed in the next chapter.

I presented renewable electricity, electro-mobility, and plant-based protein as net green substitution strategies. But even with potentially net green substitutions, it is important to not fall into the eco-efficiency trap (see Chapter 4). Cutting the GHG intensity of electricity generation or car-based transportation in half is no good if we use this as an excuse to double electricity consumption and driving. Unfortunately, global energy use, vehicle production, and driving are all still increasing, which will make it harder for these substitution strategies to reduce total environmental impact. A study published in *Nature Climate Change* in 2012 suggests that, in the past, growth in non-fossil energy use had led to shockingly small reductions in fossil fuel use.[20] Seeing that reducing fossil fuel use is the sole environmental point of renewable energy, this is extremely alarming. It is important to remember that any material, product, or technology substitution is only as green as the net environmental impact reduction it achieves.

Notes

1   Stephen Buranyi, "The Plastic Backlash: What's Behind Our Sudden Rage – And Will It Make a Difference?," *Guardian News & Media Limited*, last modified November 13, 2018, accessed July 21, 2020, www.theguardian.com/environment/2018/nov/13/the-plastic-backlash-whats-behind-our-sudden-rage-and-will-it-make-a-difference.

2   "Disposable Versus Reusable Diapers: Health, Environmental, and Economic Comparisons: Report to Procter and Gamble," *Arthur D. Little, Inc.*, (March 16, 1990), accessed January 17, 2021, https://p2infohouse.org/ref/30/29640.pdf.

3   Marin B. Hocking, "Paper Versus Polystyrene: A Complex Choice," *Science* 251, no. 4993 (February 1991): pp. 504–505, accessed July 21, 2020, DOI: 10.1126/science.251.4993.504.

4   T. N. Ligthart and A. M. M. Ansems, "Single Use Cups or Reusable (Coffee) Drinking Systems: An Environmental Comparison," *TNO*, (2007), accessed July 21, 2020, www.tno.nl/media/2915/summary-research-drinking-systems.pdf.

5   Simon Aumônier and Michael Collins, "Life Cycle Assessment of Disposable and Reusable Nappies in the UK," *Environment Agency*, (2005), accessed July 21, 2020, www.gov.uk/government/publications/disposable-and-reusable-nappies-in-the-uk-life-cycle-assessment.

6   Alexander E. Farrell et al., "Ethanol Can Contribute to Energy and Environmental Goals," *Science* 311, no. 5760 (January 2006): pp. 506–508, accessed July 21, 2020, DOI: 10.1126/science.1121416.

7   Joseph Fargione et al., "Land Clearing and the Biofuel Carbon Debt," *Science* 319, no. 5867 (February 2008): pp. 1235–1238, accessed July 21, 2020, DOI: 10.1126/science.1152747.

8   Timothy Searchinger et al., "Use of U.S. Croplands for Biofuels Increases Greenhouse Gases Through Emissions from Land-Use Change," *Science* 319, no. 5867 (February 2008): pp. 1238–1240, accessed July 21, 2020, DOI: 10.1126/science.1151861.

9   Chris Woodyard, "Ford Sees Gas Mileage Gains in New F-150 Pickups," *USA Today*, last modified November 21, 2014, accessed July 21, 2020, www.usatoday.com/story/money/cars/2014/11/21/ford-f-series-gas-mileage-aluminum/19340289/.

10 Joseph Palazzo and Roland Geyer, "Consequential Life Cycle Assessment of Automotive Material Substitution: Replacing Steel with Aluminum in North American Vehicle Production," *Environmental Impact Assessment Review* 75 (2019): pp. 47–58, accessed January 17, 2021, www.researchgate.net/deref/http%3A%2F%2Fdx.doi.org%2F10.1016%2Fj.eiar.2018.12.001.

11 "Life Cycle Assessment Harmonization," *National Renewable Energy Laboratory (NREL)*, accessed July 21, 2020, www.nrel.gov/analysis/life-cycle-assessment.html.

12 Andrew Bilich et al., "Life Cycle Assessment of Solar Photovoltaic Microgrid Systems in Off-Grid Communities," *Environmental Science and Technology* 51, no. 2 (2017): pp. 1043–1052, accessed January 17, 2021, https://doi.org/10.1021/acs.est.6b05455.

13 Vasilis Fthenakis and Hyung Chul Kim, "Land Use and Electricity Generation: A Life-Cycle Analysis," *Renewable & Sustainable Energy Reviews* 13, nos. 6–7 (2009): pp. 1465–1474, accessed January 17, 2021, https://doi.org/10.1016/j.rser.2008.09.017.

14   Rachael Nealer, David Reichmuth, and Don Anair, "Cleaner Cars from Cradle to Grave," *Union of Concerned Scientists*, (November 2015), accessed January 17, 2021, www.ucsusa.org/sites/default/files/attach/2015/11/Cleaner-Cars-from-Cradle-to-Grave-full-report.pdf; See also: Dale Hall and Nic Lutsey, "Effects of Battery Manufacturing on Electric Vehicle Life-Cycle Greenhouse Gas Emissions," *International Council on Clean Transportation*, (February 2018), accessed January 17, 2021, https://theicct.org/publications/EV-battery-manufacturing-emissions.

15   Rachael Nealer, David Reichmuth, and Don Anair, "Cleaner Cars from Cradle to Grave," *Union of Concerned Scientists*, (November 2015), accessed January 17, 2021, www.ucsusa.org/sites/default/files/attach/2015/11/Cleaner-Cars-from-Cradle-to-Grave-full-report.pdf; See also: Dale Hall and Nic Lutsey, "Effects of Battery Manufacturing on Electric Vehicle Life-Cycle Greenhouse Gas Emissions," *International Council on Clean Transportation*, (February 2018), accessed January 17, 2021, https://theicct.org/publications/EV-battery-manufacturing-emissions.

16   Alejandro Parodi et al., "The Potential of Future Foods for Sustainable and Healthy Diets," *Nature Sustainability* 1 (2018): pp. 782–789, accessed January 17, 2021, https://doi.org/10.1038/s41893-018-0189-7.

17   Jillian P. Fry et al., "Feed Conversion Efficiency in Aquaculture: Do We Measure It Correctly?," *Environmental Research Letters* 13, no. 2 (2018): p. 024017, accessed January 17, 2021, https://iopscience.iop.org/article/10.1088/1748-9326/aad007.

18   Sophie Egan, "How Much Protein Do We Need?," *The New York Times*, last modified July 28, 2017, accessed July 21, 2020, www.nytimes.com/2017/07/28/well/eat/how-much-protein-do-we-need.html;
Protein consumption data (in gram per capita per day) is available at www.fao.org/faostat/en/#data.

19   This is research from my PhD student Jason Maier, which was still unpublished at the time of writing this chapter.

20   Richard York, "Do Alternative Energy Sources Displace Fossil Fuels?," *Nature Climate Change* 2, no. 6 (2012): pp. 441–443, accessed July 21, 2020, www.nature.com/articles/nclimate1451.

9

LESS

On November 25, 2011, readers of the *New York Times* (NYT) found a full-page ad in their newspaper showing a photo of a gorgeous fleece jacket from Patagonia, the outdoor apparel company based in Ventura, California.[1] This in itself was unsurprising, given that it was Black Friday, the day after Thanksgiving and the unofficial start of the Christmas shopping season. Fueled by deep discounts, Black Friday has turned into the busiest shopping day of the year in the United States. The event has even spread to countries that don't celebrate Thanksgiving, like Germany, France, and the UK. Every year, TV footage shows masses of shoppers camping out in front of department stores, fighting over limited discounted product stock, and getting seriously injured or even killed in the process.

Right on top, in big, bold letters, the NYT ad read: DON'T BUY THIS JACKET. Now, this was highly unusual, even for a member of the outdoor equipment and apparel industry that has a track record of trying to reconcile its customers' apparent love of nature with their desire to buy stuff (outdoor gear in this case). Many of these companies were established

DOI:10.4324/9781003163060-09

by people who are outdoor enthusiasts themselves. Patagonia, which was founded and is still owned by climbing legend Yvon Chouinard, is no exception. However, Chouinard and his company are by far the most vocal in admitting and articulating the dilemma between the love of the outdoors and the environmental cost of making and consuming outdoor apparel and equipment. The ad text below the photo contains this sentence: "As is true of all the things we can make and you can buy, this jacket comes with an environmental cost higher than its price." As a consequence, the ad asks the reader "to buy less and to reflect before you spend a dime on this jacket or anything else."

The paradoxical plea to not buy its products was part of Patagonia's logical progression in its efforts to reduce the environmental impacts of its products. The company began to use recycled polyester in 1993 and switched from conventional to organic cotton in 1996. In 2005, Patagonia formed the goal to make all its clothes recyclable within the next five years. Conceding that all this was still not enough, the company launched its Common Thread Initiative in September 2011 and asked its customers "to take a formal pledge and be partners in the effort to reduce consumption."[2] The NYT ad was part of this initiative and even had a QR code at the bottom, which took the reader straight to a webpage where they could take said pledge.

Interestingly, this now-famous ad is also frequently used as a case study in brilliant marketing. *Adweek* and *AdAge* called it the "ad of the day."[3] It has even been suggested that the ad simply assuages the environmental guilt of Patagonia's customers rather than truly change their behavior. In retrospect, it does appear that Patagonia's customers either did not take or did not heed the pledge. The year 2011 turned out to be a bumper year for the company, with annual revenues jumping from 333 to over 500 million dollars.[4] Over the next six years, its revenues and profits doubled, turning Patagonia into a billion-dollar company.

The third and final pollution prevention principle is called 'less' for short. It's arguably the simplest and most powerful of the three yet also the most challenging. The basic idea is to provide a given amount of service or utility with less: Fewer products, less product use, less material, or less energy. The easiest way to explain this principle is probably with an example. Let's say the service is passenger transportation, which is typically measured in person-kilometers. A service amount of 20,000 person-kilometers means transporting 1 person a distance of 20,000 kilometers (km), or 2 people a distance of 10,000 km, etc. You get the idea. Let's assume that one person uses a vehicle that consumes 10 liters of gasoline per 100 km and lasts for 200,000 km. In that case, 20,000 person-kilometers require 2,000 liters of gasoline and one-tenth of a car. If the car mass is 2,000 kg, then one-tenth of the car is equal to 200 kg of automotive materials.

There are several ways in which the required inputs could be reduced. Imagine that we could make the car last for 400,000 km. Then 20,000 person-kilometers would require only one-twentieth of a car, or 100 kg of automotive materials. A material-intensity of 100 kg per 20,000 person-kilometers could also be achieved by halving the size of the vehicle. Such a 1,000 kg vehicle would also have a significantly reduced fuel consumption. Reducing fuel consumption is actually more important than reducing the environmental impacts of vehicle production, since 80–90% of the life cycle GHG emissions and other environmental impacts come from driving the car. Only 10–20% of the life cycle impacts are from making the car.[5] Alternative ways to reduce fuel consumption would be to make the internal combustion engine more efficient, to reduce the frontal area of the car, or to lower its drag coefficient. Carpooling, i.e. the actual sharing of rides, increases vehicle occupancy and is thus another way to reduce fuel consumption per person-kilometer. All of these measures reduce the resource-intensity of car-based passenger transportation and are thus examples of the pollution prevention principle 'less'. In this example, the aim of all reduction strategies is to provide a given amount of person-kilometers with less car, less material, less fuel.

In fact, this is exactly what happened in the United States when the oil embargo of 1973 led to escalating gasoline prices and the introduction of national fuel economy standards as part of the Energy Policy and Conservation Act of 1975. Within six years, the average weight of new cars in the United States dropped by 20%. In the same period, the average horsepower dropped by 25%. Both made the cars much more fuel efficient.[6] By 1987, the average fuel economy (the inverse of fuel consumption) had increased by almost 70%. Energy conservation measures across the globe were so successful that they ended up leading to an oil glut in the 1980s. Oil price fell from almost $40 to below $10 per barrel as a result. In the United States, the Reagan administration decided to abandon the energy conservation policies of the previous presidents. By 2004, vehicle mass was back to 1975 levels, horsepower was 55% higher than in 1975, and fuel economy was at its lowest level since 1980. While the efficiency of new car engines had continued to increase, the car companies had chosen to make bigger, heavier, and more powerful cars instead of more fuel efficient ones. This rollercoaster of gains and losses is a powerful demonstration of how effective price changes and robust policy interventions are.

After 2004, the situation turned yet again. The oil price saw a sharp and sustained rise, and California, by far the largest car market in the United States, had approved GHG vehicle emission standards under Assembly Bill 1493. In 2009, the Obama administration enacted historic new federal standards to regulate both fuel economy and GHG emissions. By 2019, the average fuel economy was almost double the value of 1975. Fantastic news but there was one glitch. Can you guess it? Between 1975 and 2019, total annual vehicle miles traveled (VMT) had increased 2.5-fold.[7] As a result, total U.S. gasoline consumption in 2019 was still 30% higher than in 1975.[8] See, fuel economy is an eco-efficiency measure, and we explored the problem with eco-efficiency in Chapter 3. Decreasing the environmental impact per person-kilometer is a great start, but it's insufficient to guarantee a net green outcome, i.e. an overall impact reduction.

So far, our car example was predicated on the assumption that the required service is a given amount of driving. A more thorough exploration of the actual need that is being met by the service can help us find additional, potentially deeper, reduction strategies. The point of passenger transportation, for example, is to provide mobility and access. We might be able to provide the same amount of access and mobility with fewer person-kilometers. This is what happened in the car-sharing case study from Chapter 6. Remember that the survey data from the UC Berkeley researchers revealed that, on average, joining a car-sharing service reduced household driving by 1,740 km per year. This means that households were able to meet all their access and mobility needs with less driving. Some of the reduction in driving was probably due to mode shifting, from cars to public transport. That would then be a substitution strategy. Generally, a net green one, by the way.

The advantage of 'less', relative to 'different' and 'again', is that the environmental impact reduction is much more directly built into the pollution prevention strategy. Why this is the case is again best explained with an illustrative example. Imagine that a company is seeking to reduce the environmental impacts from the packaging of one of its products. Let's say that the current packaging uses 100 grams of polyethylene terephthalate, better known as PET or #1 plastic. I mentioned it briefly in Chapter 7. PET is best known as the plastic that water and soda bottles are made out of, but it is also increasingly used to package all sorts of other products. What is less known is that more PET is used for textiles than for packaging. Whenever a label in your garment says polyester, it's almost certainly made from PET. But back to our case study of 100 grams of PET packaging. Let's further assume that the currently used PET is made from primary fossil resources, i.e. crude oil or natural gas. By the way, this is true for literally all plastic we currently make and use. Three of the four packaging designers tasked with this impact reduction project each identify a viable 'green' material alternative: Bio-based PET made from sugarcane, fossil-based PET with 50% post-consumer recycled content, and a composite consisting mostly of cardboard certified by the Forest Stewardship Council (FSC). Let's assume that we would need roughly 100 grams of each material. The fourth designer comes up with a radical redesign of the packaging shape, which requires the original material but only 60 grams of it. Let's assume that this mass-reduced package uses the same forming processes as the original one.

The four designers present their new packaging designs to the product line manager. She compliments each of them on their good work and then asks by how much each new design would lower the environmental impact of the packaging. I'm sure you see where I'm going with this. The first three designers would probably say something about having to do a life cycle assessment (LCA) and having to navigate a few thorny environmental trade-offs and methodological controversies. The fourth designer would simply say something like: "About 40%, I guess." See, that's the beauty of the pollution prevention strategy 'less'. It's the most direct and literal implementation of the business of less.

We spent a good deal of Chapter 8 (Different) on the complexities of environmental comparisons between different materials. We have also seen that even sophisticated LCAs, the most powerful assessment tool we currently have, are not always able to provide straightforward and actionable answers. This is less a shortcoming of LCA and more a simple reflection of the fact that all materials have significant environmental impacts. Which is why I can't get excited about the so-called bio-economy, in which increasing amounts of our materials and fuels would come from biomass rather than non-renewable resources. One example would be the sugar-cane-based PET from our earlier example. This material actually exists. Coca-Cola calls it PlantBottle™. The climate change and land use impacts of current global food production are already not sustainable, even without any PlantBottles™.[9] Just imagine by how much these impacts would increase if we were to grow biomass not just for our food and feed but also for all our materials and fuels. The combined impacts on biodiversity would be devastating.[10] Growing crops like corn and sugarcane, or anything else really, for energy is a particularly poor environmental strategy. These crops harvest sunlight and convert it into biomass using photosynthesis. Unfortunately, the energy conversion efficiency of photosynthesis is miserable. The maximum theoretical efficiency is in the low single digits. Actual efficiencies of growing fuel crops are under 1%. To put this into perspective, the energy conversion efficiencies of commercial photovoltaic (solar) panels are currently between 15% and 22%.[11] The bio-economy sounds all lush and thriving, but it would be anything but. It would create green wastelands. It is also less than clear what the GHG implications of a bio-economy would be, seeing that some biofuels and biomaterials have GHG intensities that are similar or even higher than their non-renewable competitors. It is unclear, for example, whether the carbon footprint of sugarcane-based PET is 20% lower than that of fossil-based PET or less than 10% lower.[12] Even a 20% reduction would not exactly be a game changer, especially considering that global virgin plastic production is currently growing by about 4% year over year.[13]

I did argue in Chapter 7 (Again) that the processes involved in material recycling do typically have smaller environmental footprints than those needed to make materials from virgin resources. Nonetheless, material recycling certainly has its own environmental impacts, and for some materials, like glass and paper, the difference between recycled and virgin material is more moderate than one would hope. To make things worse, recycling only really 'closes the loop' when products are both made from recycled material and recycled at the end of their lives. There are currently only a handful of products that achieve both of those things. PET is actually the perfect example. If collected and separated, PET water and soda bottles can be and are being recycled. However, their recycled content is currently close to zero. Instead, those collected post-consumer bottles are recycled into either PET fiber (better known as polyester) or so-called thermoformed trays, clamshells, and blister packs. Unfortunately, neither polyester fabric nor PET thermoforms are currently being recycled in any viable and meaningful way. So, while the polyester fleece you're wearing or the container you bought your berries in might have significant recycled content, both are destined for landfill, or worse, at the end of their lives. There is even a debate going on among LCA experts about whether the environmental benefits of recycling are attributable to recycled content or to end-of-life recycling. It is thus entirely possible that a product made from recycled material officially ends up with the carbon footprint of virgin material. In fact, 17 metal industry associations proposed this approach, which could be summarized as 'recycled content doesn't matter', for their materials in a 2007 publication in the *International Journal of Life Cycle Assessment*.[14]

So, if 'less' is the gold standard in pollution prevention, why is it not our go-to strategy? In other words, why is the most powerful pollution prevention strategy the least popular? To understand this, we first need to realize that there are two types of 'less', which play out very differently. For this, it is useful to look at a business as an organization that purchases inputs from suppliers and converts them into valuable outputs, which it then sells to its customers. Now, if you figure out a way to use less input without changing the value of a given output, companies making this output would probably love to hear about it. Using less of an input, all other things being equal, decreases environmental impact and also reduces economic cost. If the cost of the input is significant, companies have an economic incentive to use less. This is the first type of less – less input per unit output. The second type of less is to get more use or service out of each unit of output, i.e. making each unit of output go further.

Let's revisit aluminum to explore this. Aluminum is the most common metal and the third most abundant element in the earth's crust. There are ample deposits of aluminum ore all over the world. Yet, in the 19th century, aluminum used to be more expensive than gold. Napoleon III famously reserved a set of aluminum cutlery for his most special guests. Everyone else had to make do with gold cutlery. How is this possible? It turns out that the element aluminum is so reactive that it can't be extracted from its ores using traditional pyrometallurgical processes, like furnaces. Instead, aluminum ore first has to be converted to pure aluminum oxide, called alumina, through the so-called Bayer process. This generates a highly alkaline waste product called red mud. The alumina is then reduced to pure aluminum through a type of electrolysis called Hall-Héroult process, which requires large amounts of electricity. The Bayer and Hall-Héroult processes were invented right at the end of the 19th century. In the year 1904, only 10,000 tons of aluminum were produced globally. Each ton of aluminum required 47 megawatt-hours (MWh) of electricity and was therefore ridiculously expensive – $22,400 in today's dollars, to be precise. This created a big incentive to reduce the electricity demand of aluminum production. And indeed, by the year 1990, the electricity required per ton of aluminum was down to 16 MWh, a reduction by a factor of three. During the same time, the price of aluminum fell by a factor of seven, to $3,200.[15] So, here is the first type of less – less electricity input per ton of aluminum, which instantly translates into less environmental impact per ton of aluminum.

What about the second type of less – getting more use or service out of each ton of output? In this strategy, we would lower our environmental footprint simply by reducing our use of aluminum. Well, the 20th century saw an explosion of aluminum use, fueled by the dramatic drop in its price. In 1990, global primary aluminum production was 19 million tons (Mt), a 1,900-fold increase relative to the 10,000 tons in 1904. As a result, total annual electricity use for aluminum production had increased from 0.5 to 300 terawatt-hours (TWh), even though electricity input per ton of aluminum had fallen by a factor of three. A TWh is a million MWhs. By 1990, aluminum had become so cheap that it was now used for single-use beverage and food containers and then just thrown away. Okay, but that was before the Earth Summit and its plea to "find ways to halt the destruction of irreplaceable natural resources and pollution of the planet." True, but if you remember Figure 1.4 in Chapter 1, you already know that we tripled global annual production of primary aluminum since 1990. Not exactly doing more with less. You also know from the same figure that aluminum is not an outlier but the norm. To make matters worse, between 1990 and 2015, the amount of electricity required to make a ton of aluminum fell by a measly 2 MWh, from 16 MWh to 14 MWh. As a result, total electricity use for aluminum production went from 300 TWh in 1990 to 840 TWh today.[16]

Have we at least stopped throwing aluminum away – the miraculous material that used to be more precious than gold? Sadly, not. In the United States, the aluminum can collection rate even dropped from over 60% in 1990 to under 50% today, even though aluminum can scrap is worth over

$1,200 per ton.[17] At the moment, every other can made from this amazing material ends up in landfill, an incinerator, or the environment. That did not stop the media and events company GreenBiz from publishing an article at the end of 2019 called "The aluminum can: America's most successful recycling story that you've never heard."[18] I guess for GreenBiz the can is half full rather than half empty.

What does the case study of aluminum teach us about the third pollution prevention strategy? For one, we learned that the first type of less, less input per output, does happen. At the beginning of the 20th century, aluminum production was very inefficient, so there was plenty of opportunity to reduce the energy intensity of production. However, the last thirty years have only seen marginal efficiency gains. It looks like we might be running into some hard physical efficiency limits. This makes the second type of less, less output, even more important, but we are doing the exact opposite. And while we continue to increase the annual output of virgin aluminum, we keep throwing away vast amounts of it, even though the economic and environmental case for aluminum recycling is as good as it gets.

Generally speaking, the strategy of 'less physical input per physical output' has at least three serious shortcomings, which all limit its importance going forward. First, as the aluminum example illustrates, physical production processes have minimum requirements for material and energy input. As a result, this strategy will eventually run into hard physical limits, and it looks like it has done so already in many instances. Next, 'less physical input per physical output' is an eco-efficiency strategy and is thus subject to all the perils involved in relying on eco-efficiency alone. By now you are probably tired of hearing it, but it is so important that I'll say it again: Halving the input per unit output fails as net green strategy if output doubles at the same time. As discussed in Chapter 4, the rebound effect suggests that eco-efficiency even instigates growth in output, thus harboring its own undoing. Third, while this strategy is great for the company that uses the inputs in question, the suppliers of these inputs will beg to differ. While requiring less electricity for smelting will delight aluminum producers, they would not feel the same way if their customers told them that they found a way to make the same construction, automotive, and packaging products with much less aluminum. All along, the supply chain consumers of intermediate products have an economic incentive to use less, while the producers have an incentive to make and sell more. In other words, the economics of less input per output generates series of tugs-of-war rather than a coordinated impact reduction effort.

All this means that we will have to rely much more on the second type of less: Less physical output. Getting more use or service out of each unit of physical output is easily the most potent pollution prevention strategy. It enables us to reduce physical output and the associated environmental impact, while providing the same level of service or utility. It is the idea behind Patagonia's Black Friday ad and the Common Threads Initiative it was part of. The initiative encourages customers to reduce, repair, reuse, and recycle their garments and to do it in that order, which means that recycling comes last. Reduce and repair mean to get the maximum amount of service out of each piece of clothing. Unfortunately, as common sense as all this sounds, it clashes directly with the way in which we designed our business models and our economies more broadly. 'Don't buy this jacket' is based on a very astute environmental insight, but it is also a great way to put your company out of business. Well, given that your customers follow your advice, that is. Virtually all our current business models are based on selling physical goods, i.e. stuff. To make matters worse, the conviction that companies should constantly seek to increase their revenues and profits means that their aim must be to sell more stuff year over year.

At this point, we're thrown back to Jackson and Clift's observation from Chapter 5 that the profit motive encourages increased production efficiency on one hand but also increased product output on the other.[19] The work of Dahmus, discussed in Chapter 4, shows that growth in output keeps exceeding the gains in production efficiency.[20] The aluminum case study from earlier suggests that the quest for increased efficiency is running out of steam. It very much looks like we're at an impasse, unless we are prepared to completely rethink our current business models.

Let's go back to our shoe case study from Chapter 5 for a moment and assume that the company found a way to double the durability of the shoe model without affecting either cost or environmental impact. Let's further assume that the company's customers would, in fact, wear the new shoes twice as long. Extending the lifetime of a product is a poster child of the second type of less: More service per unit physical output. But we learned in Chapter 5 that the situation is more complex than it appears. If the company's customers now buy shoes at half the rate, then revenues also just went down by 50%. That may be great for the environment, but I can't see a company get excited about that, not even Patagonia. This scenario would also lead to the same indirect rebound effect described in Chapter 5, since the customers would now have large savings to spend elsewhere. To completely eliminate the possibility of rebound, the shoe with twice the lifetime would actually have to cost twice as much to make as the original shoe. In the same way, Patagonia's request to not buy their fleece jacket would only work if its customers wouldn't spend the saved money on other equally impactful products. How can companies sell less stuff without shrinking their revenues and therefore the economy as a whole? There are, of course, those who argue that shrinking the economy is unavoidable if we're serious about actual environmental impact reduction and not just fooling ourselves with eco-efficiency window dressing. In any case, is there a way to sell non-stuff? Turns out there is, and it is the subject of the next chapter.

Notes

1 Patagonia, "Don't Buy This Jacket, Black Friday and the New York Times," *The New York Times*, last modified November 25, 2011, accessed October 24, 2020, www.patagonia.com/stories/dont-buy-this-jacket-black-friday-and-the-new-york-times/story-18615.html.

2 Patagonia, "Patagonia Launches Common Threads Initiative: A Partnership With Customers to Consume Less," *PR Newswire*, last modified September 7, 2011, accessed October 24, 2020, www.prnewswire.com/news-releases/patagonia-launches-common-threads-initiative-a-partnership-with-customers-to-consume-less-129372068.html.

3 Stephen Regenold, "Redux: 'Don't Buy This Jacket'," *GearJunkie*, December 7, 2011, accessed October 24, 2020, https://gearjunkie.com/patagonia-dont-buy-this-jacket-campaign.

4 "Patagonia 2011 Sales Surpass $500 Million; CEO Explains Restructuring," *snews*, last modified May 17, 2017, accessed October 24, 2020, www.snewsnet.com/news/patagonia-2011-sales-surpass-500-million-ceo-explains-restructuring; See also: https://craft.co/patagonia/revenue.

5 Roland Geyer, "Parametric Assessment of Climate Change Impacts of Automotive Material Substitution," *Environmental Science and Technology* 42, no. 18 (2008): pp. 6973–6979, accessed January 13, 2021, https://doi.org/10.1021/es800314w.

6   "The 2019 EPA Automotive Trends Report," *U.S. Environmental Protection Agency*, accessed October 24, 2020, www.epa.gov/automotive-trends.

7   "Travel Monitoring: Historical Monthly VMT Report," *U.S. Federal Highway Administration*, accessed October 24, 2020, www.fhwa.dot.gov/policyinformation/travel_monitoring/historicvmt.cfm.

8   "Data for Automotive Trends Report," *U.S. Environmental Protection Agency*, accessed January 17, 2021, www.epa.gov/automotive-trends/data-automotive-trends-report; See also: "Overview of U.S. Petroleum Production, Imports, Exports, and Consumption," *US Bureau of Transportation*, accessed October 24, 2020, www.bts.gov/content/overview-us-petroleum-production-imports-exports-and-consumption-million-barrels-day.

9   Intergovernmental Panel on Climate Change, *Climate Change and Land: An IPCC Special Report on Climate Change, Desertification, Land Degradation, Sustainable Land Management, Food Security and Greenhouse Gas Fluxes in Terrestrial Ecosystems*, edited by H. -O. Pörtner et al. (Geneva: Intergovernmental Panel on Climate Change, 2019), www.ipcc.ch/report/srccl/.

10 David R. Williams et al., "Proactive Conservation to Prevent Habitat Losses to Agricultural Expansion," *Nature Sustainability*, (2020), accessed January 17, 2021, https://doi.org/10.1038/s41893-020-00656-5.

11 John Andrews and Nick Jelley, *Energy Science*, 3rd ed. (Oxford: Oxford University Press, 2017); See also: "Champion Photovoltaic Module Efficiency Chart," *National Renewable Energy Laboratory*, accessed January 17, 2021, www.nrel.gov/pv/module-efficiency.html.

12 Dan Leif, "After PlantBottle Claims Are Knocked, Coke Opens up on Carbon Stats," *Plastics Recycling Update*, last modified August 9, 2013, accessed January 17, 2021, https://resource-recycling.com/plastics/2013/08/09/plantbottle-claims-knocked-coke-opens-carbon-stats/.

13 Roland Geyer, Jenna R. Jambeck, and Kara Lavender Law, "Production, Use, and Fate of All Plastics Ever Made," *Science Advances* 3, no. 7 (2017), https://advances.sciencemag.org/content/3/7/e1700782.

14 John Atherton, "Declaration by the Metals Industry on Recycling Principles," *International Journal of Life Cycle Assessment* 12 (2006): pp. 59–60, accessed January 17, 2021, https://link.springer.com/article/10.1065/lca2006.11.283.

15   Thomas D. Kelly et al., "Historical Statistics for Mineral and Material Commodities in the United States," *United States Geological Survey*, (2015), accessed January 17, 2021, www.usgs.gov/centers/nmic/historical-statistics-mineral-and-material-commodities-united-states;   Jeffrey   B. Dahmus, "Can Efficiency Improvements Reduce Resource Consumption? A Historical Analysis of Ten Activities," *Journal of Industrial Ecology* 18, no. 6 (2014): pp. 883–897, accessed July 21, 2020, https://doi.org/10.1111/jiec.12110.

16   "Life Cycle Inventory Data and Environmental Metrics for the Primary Aluminum Industry: 2015 Data," *International Aluminium Institute*, (June 2017), accessed January 13, 2021, www.world-aluminium.org/media/filer_public/2017/06/28/lca_report_2015_final.pdf.

17   "The Aluminum Can Advantage," *The Aluminum Association*, accessed October 24, 2020, www.aluminum.org/aluminum-can-advantage; See also: "Aluminum Can Recycling Rates (1990–2010)," *Container Recycling Institute*, accessed October 24, 2020, www.container-recycling.org/index.php/76-aluminum/data-archive/208-aluminum-can-recycling-rates-1990-2010.

18   Gina Lee, "The Aluminum Can: America's Most Successful Recycling Story That You've Never Heard," last modified November 15, 2019, accessed October 24, 2020, www.greenbiz.com/article/aluminum-can-americas-most-successful-recycling-story-youve-never-heard.

19   Tim Jackson and Roland Clift, "Where's the Profit in Industrial Ecology?," *Journal of Industrial Ecology* 2, no. 1 (1998): pp. 3–5, accessed July 21, 2020, https://doi.org/10.1162/jiec.1998.2.1.3.

20   Jeffrey B. Dahmus, "Can Efficiency Improvements Reduce Resource Consumption? A Historical Analysis of Ten Activities," *Journal of Industrial Ecology* 18, no. 6 (2014): pp. 883–897, accessed July 21, 2020, https://doi.org/10.1111/jiec.12110.

10

LABOR, NOT MATERIALS

In 2016, Trevor Zink and I published a paper called "There is no such thing as a green product."[1] The title was born from our growing frustration with the then prevailing and still persisting obsession with 'green' materials, products, and technologies. This preoccupation seems to be bound up in multiple layers of misconception. One of them is the idea that selling or buying a green product in and of itself somehow generates environmental benefits. Unless you just sold or bought something akin to a tree, this is, of course, nonsense. All material goods have environmental impacts. A Toyota Prius may get 50 or more miles per gallon (mpg) of gasoline, but that alone does not make it green. There is nothing green about a Prius if you buy it in addition to the pickup truck and the SUV already in your driveway. That Prius is also not green if you didn't own a car before and used to walk, bike, or take public transport instead. You may argue that you could have bought an SUV instead of a Prius, but the point is that any car ownership will increase your transportation impacts, regardless of the model you choose. A Prius can facilitate environmental impact reduction

DOI:10.4324/9781003163060-10

if you drive it instead of your previous 25 mpg vehicle, while not using your new fuel efficiency as an excuse to drive more. And even then, you still need to make sure that the way in which you spend your fuel savings does not dampen your emission reductions by too much. All these caveats form the motivation behind the concept of 'net green', which Trevor and I introduced in that 2016 paper and I dedicated Chapter 6 of this book to.

A net green analysis inventories all the environmentally relevant consequences of an activity, such as buying a car or installing solar panels on the roof of your house. If your new solar panels do not decrease your consumption of grid electricity, they are not net green. And even if your overall electricity consumption stays exactly the same, the greenness of the solar panels still depends on the environmental profile of the grid electricity they displace. It therefore makes a big difference whether you live in British Columbia, where 94% of the grid electricity is from renewable resources, or Wyoming, where 88% is from coal.[2]

Greenness is thus a relative property and says as much about the product it is meant to describe as it says about the one that is meant to be displaced. I would argue that not infrequently the potential greenness of a new product or technology is mostly a reflection of the 'brownness' of the incumbent. Using lead as antiknock in gasoline, DDT as insecticide, or CFCs as propellants in spray cans were such bad ideas that pretty much any alternative was bound to be an improvement. Incandescent lightbulbs convert only around 5% of the electricity they consume into light.[3] The rest is emitted as waste heat. They're really heaters that give off a bit of light, so it's unsurprising that we found greener artificial lighting technologies. Internal combustion vehicles convert 20–25% of the fuel energy into work at the wheel.[4] If we assume that a 2,000 kg car carries an 80 kg person, then less than 1% of the fuel energy ends up moving the passenger. A Prius increases this value to maybe 2%. Does that make the Prius green or just a bit less brown than a conventional car?

Climate scientists have told us for decades now that burning fossil fuels worth hundreds of Exajoules (580 in 2019 alone) and thus emitting billions of tons of carbon dioxide every year (around 34 in 2019) will destabilize the earth's climate.[5] Large scale use of fossil energy turned out to be such a bad idea, that wind and solar energy may well be called green or at least dramatically less brown. There is no doubt that a radical shift from fossil to renewable energy sources, together with the required electrification of previously fossil-powered energy services, is urgently required. Yet even a completely renewable energy system would still come with a hefty environmental price tag. It would require large amounts of metals and other elements and large amounts of land, especially if we keep increasing our demand for energy services. It's an illusion to think that we could harvest 600 Exajoules worth of renewable energy without significant environmental impacts. Also, as a reality check, keep in mind that since the Earth Summit in Rio, we increased our non-fossil share of global energy consumption by a meagre 3% (from 13 to 16).[6]

When it comes to materials, even defining the meaning of less brown becomes a challenge, let alone defining green. As illustrated by the various examples in the previous chapters, all materials have significant environmental impacts. The most likely outcome of switching materials is to shift environmental impacts rather than to reduce them across the board. This makes the notion of a green material a bit of an oxymoron. Environmental impacts per unit of material did decrease over the decades, so we did manage to make most materials less brown than they used to be. But we have already seen that these eco-efficiency efforts were outpaced by the growth in total material use. It also means that further increasing the eco-efficiency of material production will become ever more difficult.

There is one resource, though, that has no environmental impacts whatsoever. Labor. By labor, I mean any and all kind of value-adding human activity in production, maintenance, repair, and service provision more broadly. Think about it. We eat, drink, and breathe, whether we work or not. As a result, substituting energy or material resources with labor is guaranteed to reduce environmental impacts. In other words, using labor instead of materials or energy is always net green since labor has no environmental impacts. Sweeping up leaves with a broom is greener than using a leaf blower, regardless of what materials the blower is made of and whether it is gas- or solar-powered. Delivering documents via bike courier is greener than using a car, even if it's a Prius or Tesla. Using labor instead of materials or energy is also almost guaranteed to cost more. That fact is typically seen as a major drawback of this substitution strategy. However, as we pointed out in Chapter 5, such a cost increase further reduces environmental impact, since it avoids the environmental impact of spending the money otherwise. We called this a reverse rebound effect since it works like an indirect rebound effect but with opposite signs. At the end of Chapter 5, we hypothesized about a change in shoe production that decreased environmental impact but increased production cost. Let's imagine this is due to a switch from energy-intensive processes to skilled labor. The switch itself is already net green, but the cost increase further reduces environmental impact.

I know what you're thinking now. We just spent the last several hundred years doing the exact opposite. Beginning with the industrial revolution, we have been substituting labor with energy and materials. While this giant substitution project generated unheard-of economic wealth and technical capabilities, it is also the driver behind the multiple environmental crises we are now confronted with, including climate change, biodiversity loss, and widespread environmental contamination with toxic or hazardous substances. By relentlessly substituting labor with materials and energy, we not only overshot the carrying capacity of this planet but also the usefulness of this substitution. Instead of falsely hoping that green products and technologies can save us all on their own, I propose to resubstitute some of that lost labor. The beauty of this proposal is that it would not just further environmental but also social sustainability goals.

Now that we know that labor is the one production input that is truly without environmental impact, it is worthwhile to revisit the three pollution prevention principles and explore how they relate to labor. Let's begin with reuse and recycling, or 'again' for short. The main environmental motivation behind reuse and recycling is the fact that secondary production processes have lower environmental impacts than primary production activities. A major reason for this is that recovering value from end-of-life products requires fewer material and energy inputs than primary production but more labor. The most material- and energy-intensive production processes are the ones right at the beginning of the value chain, where natural resources are extracted and converted into valuable materials. Recycling avoids these extraction and conversion processes and instead requires labor during collection, sorting, and pre-processing of end-of-life products. While this increased labor-intensity increases the economic cost of recycling, it is also a reason behind its environmental advantage. If we recover not just materials, as done in recycling, but entire components or even products, this effect becomes even more pronounced. The material- and energy-intensive processes of making, shaping, and finishing materials into components and assembling them into products are replaced by labor-intensive activities such as disassembly, inspection, testing, and repair. The potential environmental benefits of reuse and recycling are thus a function of the material- and energy-intensity of the processes that are avoided and the labor-intensity of the processes that are required instead. The higher up in the value chain the supply loop is closed, the more pronounced is the effect of this substitution. For this reason, product reuse tends to have the highest environmental potential, followed by component reuse, while recycling lands at the bottom of the hierarchy.

The second pollution prevention principle is material, product, and technology substitution, or 'different' for short. There is no obvious relationship between this strategy and labor. At the risk of making a tautological statement: All primary material production is material- and energy-intensive. It is thus unsurprising that switching materials typically shifts rather than fundamentally reduces environmental burdens. Product and technology substitution has true environmental potential only when the old product or technology is inefficient or has a very specific and unacceptable type of environmental impact. Examples from Chapter 8 that fall into the first category are electro-mobility and plant-based protein. Electric powertrains are three to four times as efficient as powertrains with an internal combustion engine.[7] And it is obviously much more efficient to eat plants directly rather than use them to raise animals. Into the second category fall the aforementioned examples of lead, DDT, CFCs, and fossil fuels.

The final and most important pollution prevention principle is 'less', which can either mean less physical input per physical output or simply less physical output. Skilled labor, knowledge, and expertise can help to get better and more durable products out of a given amount of material and energy input. They can also help to get more service out of a given amount of product output, through maintenance, repair, upgrades, and many other value-adding services.

Labor doesn't even have to substitute materials or energy in order to make products greener. All a company has to do is add more labor to the existing inputs. This makes the cost of the product go up, while its environmental impact stays the same. As a result, the overall environmental impact of household spending is reduced, thanks to the reverse rebound effect. To be fair, this only works if households accept the price increase rather than go and look for cheaper products.

A case study will help us to explore this in more detail. Let's assume that a fleece jacket, like the one Patagonia doesn't want you to buy, costs $80 and has a GHG footprint of 30 kg CO_2e. A typical eco-efficiency effort would look for ways to reduce the carbon footprint of the jacket, for example by changing its material. A win-win eco-efficiency effort would look for ways to reduce the carbon footprint that also reduces production cost. This could be achieved, for example, by reducing material and energy waste along the supply chain. However, as discussed in Chapter 5, any cost reduction would come with a rebound effect. So, let's assume that the apparel company finds a cost-neutral way to reduce the carbon footprint by one-third. Now, every dollar spent on a fleece jacket generates only 0.25 kg CO_2e instead of 0.38. Unfortunately, sustainability experts in the apparel industry will readily tell you that finding a way to reduce the GHG intensity of apparel production by 33% is extremely difficult, if not impossible.

Let's assume instead that the company adds $40 worth of labor to the jacket. The resulting $120 jacket also has a GHG intensity of 0.25 kg CO_2e per dollar. It is greener than the original version due to the reverse rebound effect of a cost increase accompanied by zero environmental impact. Added to this environmental benefit is the economic benefit of providing $40 worth of employment. This could be achieved through labor-intensive design changes to the jacket such as stitching, trim, or other details. It could also be done in the form of much-needed wage increases all along the global apparel supply chain. Like many other sectors, the apparel industry is routinely accused of unfairly exploiting the vast wage differences that exist on the global labor market. Again, all this requires the willing support of apparel customers, i.e. all of us.

On my mother's side, I come from a family of tailors, so I grew up witnessing firsthand the hard work that goes into every single piece of clothing. For me, handmade tailored clothing was not some extravagant luxury but simply how my grandparents and my uncle made their living. I am always taken aback by today's low apparel prices and not at all surprised that they are achieved at the expense of both workers and nature.

I started this chapter by looking for ways to make products greener and found labor as the greenest of all production inputs. Increasing the labor content in products, say through raising excessively low wages, is thus a powerful net green strategy. It also happens to further social sustainability goals. Vice versa, advocating for fair wages is obviously a very important objective in and of itself. It just also turns out to be a more effective way to reduce environmental impact than looking for that mythical green material or production technology. Truly increasing social and environmental sustainability at the same time, now there's a win-win I can get behind. As mentioned twice already, this only works if customers can be convinced that this is a worthwhile way to spend their money. I will leave this to the marketing and communications experts, but telling customers that they can reduce their environmental impact and increase social justice by purchasing this beautiful but pricier fleece jacket should be a satisfying task. A story worth crafting and telling.

Most of us live in economies that generate unsustainable amounts of environmental impacts and, at the same time, increasingly fail to provide sufficient and adequate employment. That shifting production inputs from materials and energy to labor can address both issues simultaneously is an attractive idea. It would be naïve, though, to think that simply pointing this out to companies and households would bring about the desired change, especially if we consider that we have been moving in the opposite direction for such a long time. Effecting a noticeable shift towards more or better-paid labor is likely to require robust policy support. One possible intervention is called ecological tax reform.[8] The main ideas behind ecological tax reform are at least as old as the Earth Summit in Rio. In fact, the central tenet of taxing an economic bad, such as pollution, in order to internalize its cost goes back all the way to 1920, when it was proposed by British economist Arthur Pigou.[9] The reasoning behind ecological tax reform goes roughly like this: While we are overusing the natural environment as source of materials and energy and as sink for wastes and emissions, we are underusing labor. One reason for this is that the former is too cheap, while the latter is too expensive. Ecological tax reform addresses both issues by shifting taxation from labor to natural resource use and pollution. It is typically designed to be revenue-neutral, i.e. there is no net change in tax revenue. One popular specific proposal is to tax fossil energy use or carbon emissions, while at the same time reducing income tax by the same amount. An important feature of ecological tax reform is the generation of a 'double dividend'. It discourages natural resource use and pollution by making them more expensive and encourages increased use of labor by reducing its cost. During the last three decades, several countries tinkered with ecological tax reform, but it has yet to be implemented widely and decisively. While ecological tax reform has considerable support in principle, it has been met with opposition in practice. Criticism and concerns include potential negative impacts on competitiveness, trade, low-income households, and equity more broadly. The devil, as always, is certainly in the details. And, of course, proposing a new tax is a nonstarter anywhere where any tax is considered evil.

I started this book with the United Nations (UN) Conference on Environment and Development, or Earth Summit, in 1992. The UN is still trying to get the world off its unsustainable path, now with 17 sustainable development goals (SDGs for short), set in 2015 by the UN General Assembly.[10] The goals range from reducing income inequality and attaining decent work for all to combating climate change and halting biodiversity loss. They basically list the requirements for people and planet to thrive. I believe that the best thing we could do to move towards these goals would be a massive shift from producing and consuming physical stuff to paying each other for our time, skills, and knowledge. In other words, I convinced myself that labor, rather than green products or materials, holds the key to social and environmental sustainability. Every dollar spent on labor can't be spent on stuff and thus generates the double dividend of increasing employment and decreasing environmental impact. So, if labor is the ultimate green production input, the ultimate ecolabel might not contain the carbon or water footprint of the product but rather its labor content and a credible assurance of fair wages.

Let's dream for a second here at the end of this chapter and imagine that we would all insist that every single person involved in the production of everything we consume was paid a fair wage. Yes, almost everything would become quite a bit more expensive. But think about the upside. We would consume fewer things, which would massively reduce our environmental footprint. At the same time, we could feel really good about everything we produce and consume. If the idea of a fair wage for everyone sounds crazy, just think about what this says about us. It means that we are okay with exploitation of labor, i.e. people, just so we can continue to have $100 laptops, $10 T-shirts, $3 punnets of strawberries, and $1 chocolate bars. I just don't think that's truly who we are.

Notes

1   Trevor Zink and Roland Geyer, "There Is No Such Thing as a Green Product," *Stanford Social Innovation Review*, (2016): pp. 26–31, accessed December 4, 2020, https://ssir.org/articles/entry/there_is_no_such_thing_as_a_green_product#.

2   "Provincial and Territorial Energy Profiles – British Columbia," *Canada Energy Regulator*, accessed December 4, 2020, www.cer-rec.gc.ca/en/data-analysis/energy-markets/provincial-territorial-energy-profiles/provincial-territorial-energy-profiles-british-columbia.html; "Wyoming State Profile and Energy Estimates," *U.S. Energy Information Administration*, accessed December 4, 2020, www.eia.gov/state/analysis.php?sid=WY.

3   Roger A. Hinrichs and Merlin Kleinbach, *Energy: Its Use and the Environment*, 5th ed. (Boston, MA: Brooks/Cole, 2013).

4   Roland Geyer and Donald E. Malen, "Parsimonious Powertrain Modeling for Environmental Vehicle Assessments: Part 1-Internal Combustion Vehicles," *International Journal of Life Cycle Assessment* 25 (2020): pp. 1566–1575, accessed January 17, 2021, https://doi.org/10.1007/s11367-020-01774-0.

5   "Statistical Review of World Energy 2020," *British Petroleum*, (2020), accessed December 4, 2020, www.bp.com/en/global/corporate/energy-economics/statistical-review-of-world-energy.html.

6   "Statistical Review of World Energy 2020," *British Petroleum*, (2020), accessed December 4, 2020, www.bp.com/en/global/corporate/energy-economics/statistical-review-of-world-energy.html.

7   Ronald Geyer and Donald E. Malen, "Parsimonious Powertrain Modeling for Environmental Vehicle Assessments: Part 2-Electric Vehicles," *International Journal of Life Cycle Assessment* 25 (2020): pp. 1576–1585, accessed January 17, 2021, https://doi.org/10.1007/s11367-020-01775-z.

8   Anselm Görres, Henner Ehringhaus, and Ernst Ulrich von Weizsäcker, *Der Weg zur Ökologischen Steuerreform* (München, Germany: Olzog Verlag, 1994).

9   Steve Bernow et al., "Ecological Tax Reform," *BioScience* 48, no. 3 (1998): pp. 193–196, accessed January 17, 2021, https://pdxscholar.library.pdx.edu/iss_pub/1/.

10 Department of Economic and Social Affairs: Sustainable Development, "The 17 Goals," *United Nations*, accessed January 17, 2021, https://sdgs.un.org/goals.

11

NET GREEN FOR BUSINESS

What is the role of business? I think it is fair to say that Milton Friedman's (in)famous statement from 1970 "the social responsibility of business is to increase its profits" is falling out of favor.[1] So is its modern-day variant which states that the sole responsibility of business is to its shareholders and that shareholders demand that profits be maximized.

One definition that I really like, due to its simplicity and lack of normative judgement, is this: "The fundamental role of business has remained relatively constant: providing the goods and services that people need or want." This definition was written in 2014 by Yvan Allaire as Chair of the Global Agenda Council on the Role of Business.[2] Allaire then goes on to advocate for a return to the view that companies have responsibilities to all its stakeholders, not just its shareholders. The term stakeholders is used here in the broadest possible sense. It includes customers, employees, supply chain partners, society as a whole, and even the natural environment.

Allaire is not alone in this view but part of a larger movement. I mentioned in Chapter 5 that the Business Roundtable, an association of American

DOI:10.4324/9781003163060-11

CEOs, officially changed its definition of the purpose of a company in August 2019.[3] It was a very visible and official move away from shareholder primacy and towards corporate responsibility to all stakeholders. The new statement explicitly mentions compensating employees fairly, dealing fairly and ethically with suppliers, and protecting the environment. Unless this is pure lip service, I seem to be much closer aligned with America's CEOs than I imagined.

The movement away from shareholder primacy has even reached the legal realm. Since 2010, U.S. businesses can incorporate as a so-called benefit corporation.[4] This legal structure turns the pursuit of social and environmental goals, in addition to financial ones, into legally defined and defensible objectives of the company. In addition to this legal structure, companies can also join the third-party B Corp certification program, which assesses the progress towards their social and environmental goals every year. In late 2020, over 3,600 businesses were certified B Corps.

The apparel company Patagonia has been a certified B Corp since 2011, but you may not be surprised to hear that their stated purpose now goes quite a bit further than adding a few social and environmental goals. In 2018, Patagonia changed its mission statement from "Build the best product, cause no unnecessary harm, use business to inspire and implement solutions to the environmental crisis" to "We're in business to save our home planet." Asked for the reason behind this change, founder Yvon Chouinard said this: "It's because we're destroying the planet, and it's gotten so dire that we have to do something about it."[5]

So, if the fundamental role of business is to provide the goods and services that people need or want, what is the role of business on a planet in peril? My answer in Chapter 6 was this: To provide for everyone while dramatically reducing the environmental impact of doing so. This is the essence of the business of less.

As you know from previous chapters, after decades of conflict between industry and environmentalists, the 1992 Earth Summit firmly established the view that business could and should play an active role in the pursuit of sustainability. However, back then it was still unthinkable to question the corporate gospel of shareholder primacy and profit maximization. The resulting challenge was therefore how to reconcile it with the United Nations' urgent call for environmental impact reduction. The Business Council for Sustainable Development was explicitly established to explore how this could be achieved and did not take long to settle on eco-efficiency and win-win as the main tools.[6]

Eco-efficiency assures us that we can significantly reduce environmental impact while continuing to pursue economic growth. Win-win asserts that environmental impact reduction is very much compatible with profit maximization. Taken together this conveniently meant that there was no need to question either economic growth or profit maximization. Eco-efficiency and win-win had now nearly thirty years to prove themselves, and I spent a significant part of this book to illustrate how they have failed us. I proposed in Chapter 6 that we discard them as our guiding principles for corporate sustainability. Just focusing on reducing the environmental impact per unit output without questioning the type and quantity of output will not take us off our unsustainable path. To finally get off this path, we also have to stop telling ourselves that businesses will never have to make trade-offs between serious environmental impact reduction and profit maximization.

Just to be clear: I am not saying that reducing the environmental impact of a given output is useless. I am saying that, for all the reasons given in Chapters 4 and 9, eco-efficiency has fallen far short of what we have to achieve and will continue to do so. I am also not demanding that businesses cease to make a profit. Profit is the income of the business owners and thus necessary, of course. Unless the owners are independently wealthy, that is. It is the constant conflation of making a profit and maximizing it that is the problem. In addition, we have to stop insisting that environmental impact reduction needs to piggyback on the profit motive and cannot be a business goal in its own right. It can be, even legally now, and it must be since our planet's future depends on it.

In 1999, business strategy scholar Forest Reinhardt famously said that managers should look at environmental problems as business issues, that is, purely through the lenses of profits and shareholder value.[7] After twenty years of chafing against this statement, I officially and publicly disagree. The motivation for the pursuit of environmental issues should be the environmental issue itself, not the prospect of increased profitability. Equally important, however, is a commitment to dramatically reduce environmental impact, not just to slow its growth. Therefore, out with eco-efficiency and win-win, and in with net green.

The net green concept is explicitly defined to avoid those two pitfalls. It refocuses attention on environmental sustainability as a goal in its own right. Hence the word green. It also emphasizes that the goal is absolute, not relative, impact reduction. Hence the word net. To determine whether a business activity, such as changing an existing product or launching a new service, is net green, all significant environmental implications need to be identified and assessed. This is the net green analysis introduced in Chapter 6 and illustrated with the car-sharing case study. Whether done quantitatively or qualitatively, in great detail or on the back of an envelope, the most important job of a net green analysis is to not leave anything significant out, even if it is marred by uncertainty. The key questions it asks are these: What will the net environmental consequences of this business activity be, and how uncertain are they?

I dedicated the entire previous chapter to labor as a net green strategy due to its high certainty of net environmental benefits. Labor is the one production input with no environmental impact. Substituting any material or energy input with labor will therefore always be net green. Thanks to the reverse rebound effect, adding labor is always net green, even if it does not displace any material or energy inputs. That way a store-bought sandwich containing $2 worth of ingredients and $6 worth of labor becomes greener than making that same sandwich by yourself. In fact, any labor-based business model is net green since it helps to redirect household spending away from stuff and towards low- or zero-impact services. I would thus argue that haircuts, music lessons, exercise classes, and massages are greener than 'green' products, even though none of these services tend to feature in the business sustainability literature. The basic mistake behind this omission is that the literature focuses entirely on finding equivalent but lower-impact substitutes for high-impact products or services. However, households don't simply choose between alternative products offering equivalent services. All discretionary household spending could go to wildly different product and service categories. The choice could, for example, be between a restaurant visit and an electronic gadget. Therefore, every dollar spent on haircuts, music lessons, exercise classes, and massages cannot be spent on environmentally impactful stuff and is thus net green. In fact, the greenest economy of all would be one in which we just pay each other for our time rather than making and selling stuff to each other. This would be after we have taken care of our material needs, of course.

Another key net green strategy for businesses is the willingness to examine and change their business models. For too many businesses, corporate sustainability means trying to lower the environmental impact of their products and services without ever questioning the fundamental suitability of these products and services. Not only does such an attitude severely limit the opportunities for meaningful net green activities but on a planet in peril it can even backfire economically. Volkswagen comes to mind here. Until very recently, Volkswagen and the rest of the German car industry were determined to stick to internal combustion vehicles, while attempting to make them greener. As a result, Volkswagen not only (almost) missed the electro-mobility revolution but also caused the major emission cheating scandal known as 'Dieselgate'.[8]

Exxon Mobil may become another example. While Exxon Mobil has considerable in-house life cycle assessment expertise, it is completely committed to fossil fuels and has so far made no attempts to diversify its energy portfolio. Right now, it looks like the renewable energy transition will take place without them. In 2020, fossil fuel consumption declined for the first time in modern history, while wind and solar power officially became the cheapest source of electricity.[9] In 2020, Exxon Mobil not only had losses of $22 billion but also lost one-third of its share price and its membership of the Dow Jones Industrial Average.[10]

Chapter 9 taught us that primary aluminum production has reached a level of efficiency that makes further impact reductions very challenging. This is more or less true for all materials. Nevertheless, all primary material industries are sticking to their business model of producing and selling ever-increasing amounts of material. This is as unsustainable as internal combustion engines and fossil fuels. But just like many in the car and fossil fuel industries keep throwing around terms like 'clean coal' and 'clean diesel', many primary material producers started to promise carbon-neutral materials. Net green analyses would show that none of this would be possible on a global level. To begin with, the renewable energy and biomass requirements would be completely overwhelming. Environmental sustainability will remain a pipe dream until all industries, including material producers, start to rethink their business models. Rather than promising materials that have no environmental impact, producers need to find ways to decouple their revenues from virgin material output.

Now, all business activities, even environmentally motivated ones, are virtually guaranteed to generate their own environmental impacts. Two things need to happen for a business activity to be net green: First, they need to lead to environmental impact reductions. This can potentially happen anywhere: within the boundaries of the business, in its supply chain, or somewhere else entirely. Second, these impact reductions need to be significantly larger than the generated impacts. To be able to judge the greenness of a business activity, all significant increases and reductions therefore need to be identified and assessed. Some will be easy to quantify with high certainty. Others might be potentially large but very uncertain. The second type of impacts are just as important as the first ones. Ignoring them would make life easier but would not help businesses become more sustainable. It is worthwhile to work through a few examples to see how all of this can play out.

We start with a substitution example that initially seems very simple. Company A switches its electricity input from coal-based power to hydropower. Based on the GHG numbers in Chapter 8, we would expect the carbon footprint of the company's electricity to go down by two orders of magnitude. However, if the hydroelectricity comes from an existing plant with fixed capacity, it is quite likely that a previous hydropower customer now lost her contract and has to switch to another source. If that alternative source is coal, there would be no GHG reductions whatsoever, just a shifting around of sources. To avoid this from happening, Company A should make sure that its renewable electricity comes from additional generation capacity that isn't spoken for yet, like a new wind park or solar farm. For this substitution example to become truly net green, the coal-based power output that Company A no longer uses needs to be permanently curtailed rather than used by someone else. So, ideally, Company A should actively support an overall reduction of fossil-based power generation, not just look for renewable power for itself.

Here is another substitution example that is trickier than it first appears. Company B switches from producing and selling incandescent to LED lighting. The luminous efficacy of LEDs is about ten times higher than that of incandescent lighting.[11] LCAs consistently show that this increase in lighting efficiency far outweighs the fact that LEDs have higher production impacts than incandescent lighting. Yet again, LED lighting is only net green if it sufficiently reduces the use of conventional lighting technology. Therefore, Company B should focus on lighting products designed to replace existing artificial lighting and to reduce overall lighting use instead of trying to find new lighting markets and expand existing ones.

Let's have a look at a recycling example. Company C considers switching its entire leisure and active wear from virgin to recycled nylon. With around 9 kg CO_2e per kg, nylon has the highest GHG intensity of all synthetic fibers.[12] The GHG footprint of mechanically recycled industrial nylon waste shows a tenfold reduction.[13] Fibers from chemically recycled retired fishing nets, on the other hand, offer only moderate GHG reductions. What should Company C choose? Mechanical recycling of industrial nylon waste does not just have low environmental impact; it is also not difficult. In other words, it isn't really waste and thus recycled and used no matter what. Total output is also a fixed fraction of virgin nylon production, which means that there is only a limited amount to go around. So, if Company C switches from virgin to postindustrial recycled nylon, other companies would have to switch the other way round. The result is no environmental benefit whatsoever. In contrast, if the retired fishing nets are not collected for recycling, they will end up in landfills, open dumps, or maybe even in the ocean. Producing and using nylon from retired fishing nets thus has the double benefits of reducing GHG emissions and avoiding disposal.

Another recycling example: Fruit and vegetable farmers routinely cover their fields with plastic film, also known as synthetic mulch, to suppress weeds and improve growing conditions. However, at the end of each growing season, they are left with large piles of plastic waste contaminated with soil and moisture. Farming Company D has found recycling Company R that agrees to take its mulch film waste for a charge considerably lower than the landfill fee that Company D is currently paying. Does this cost reduction opportunity also reduce environmental impact? In order to answer this question, we need to compare the impacts of the recycling process with the impacts that are avoided. For that, it is necessary to know what kind of recycled materials the mulch film waste is turned into and what materials this recycled output is able to displace. If the recycled mulch film is unlikely to displace any material, landfill would actually be the less impactful choice.

Now, let's revisit these four examples from the perspective of the third pollution prevention strategy: Less. Well, for Company A, the obvious thing to do is to look for opportunities to reduce its electricity consumption. Any resulting cost savings should be used in ways that avoid or minimize rebound. Maybe it is possible to substitute some of the company's energy consumption with labor. Company B's net green challenge is to avoid unsustainable growth in artificial lighting use. One possibility could be to add consulting services to its business, which help customers achieve their lighting objectives with minimal amounts of artificial lighting. That way, Company B could grow its business without having to sell more lighting. You will spot two by-now-familiar themes here. One is to help customers fulfill their needs with less physical product, similar to the car-sharing example. The other is to sell labor, here in the form of expertise, instead of physical goods.

Apparel Company C could reduce its reliance on making and selling new clothes by adding reuse and repair to its business model. This would be another example of selling labor instead of materials so that customers can meet their needs (in this case clothing) with fewer physical goods (in this instance clothes). Incidentally, Patagonia started doing just that in 2013, when it started its Worn Wear program. Here, the net green challenge is to make sure that reuse and repair activities reduce the sales of new clothes as this is the sole source of environmental benefit. A resulting necessary condition is that the reuse and repair business is viable on its own and doesn't need to be subsidized by revenue from new clothes sales.

The big question for Farming Company D is whether it could reduce its reliance on synthetic mulch film. Obviously, there were reasons to start using it in the first place, such as reducing cost and enhancing growing conditions. Simply doing away with synthetic mulch film would also remove these advantages. But to what extent could labor be used as a substitute for mulch film? Are there alternative, lower impact mulch materials that require an acceptable amount of additional labor? Should we even consider growing fruit and vegetable without soil altogether, something known as hydroponics?

On a planet in peril, the role of companies is not just to provide goods and services but also to dramatically reduce the environmental impact of doing so. Just slowing down the growth of environmental impact as we have done, to some extent, during the last thirty years is not an option anymore. The pollution prevention strategies of 'different', 'again', 'less', and 'labor, not materials' are there to help companies identify potentially net green business activities. A net green analysis then takes a hard look at their actual net green potential. The net green concept replaces the wishful thinking of win-win and eco-efficiency with a set of sometimes difficult but always vital questions. There is no alternative for businesses that want to be, as the slightly stale saying goes, part of the solution instead of being part of the problem. Yet even the most willing and ambitious company will need the strong support of both policy makers and households. Bold and deft policy interventions are needed to make sure that the most promising net green business activities are economically sustainable. And households are the ones that need to purchase those net green products and services. A lot has been said about companies having to walk their sustainability talk. The same is true for households.

Notes

1   Milton Friedman, "The Social Responsibility of Business Is to Increase Its Profits," *The New York Times Magazine,* last modified September 13, 1970, accessed January 3, 2021, http://umich.edu/~thecore/doc/Friedman.pdf.

2   Yvan Allaire, "What Is the Role of Business?," *World Economic Forum*, last modified January 22, 2014, accessed January 3, 2020, www.weforum.org/agenda/2014/01/role-business/.

3   "Business Roundtable Redefines the Purpose of a Corporation to Promote 'An Economy That Serves All Americans'," *Business Roundtable*, last modified August 19, 2019, accessed January 3, 2021, www.businessroundtable.org/business-roundtable-redefines-the-purpose-of-a-corporation-to-promote-an-economy-that-serves-all-americans.

4   "Benefit Corporation," *Benefit Corporation*, accessed January 3, 2021, https://benefitcorp.net/.

5   "What's at Stake Is the Future of Humankind: An Interview with Yvon Chouinard," *Patagonia*, accessed January 3, 2021, www.patagonia.com/stories/whats-at-stake-is-the-future-of-humankind/story-72130.html.

6   Stephan Schmidheiny, *Changing Course, a Global Business Perspective on Development and Business* (Cambridge, MA: Massachusetts Institute of Technology Press, 1992).

7   Forest Reinhardt, "Bringing the Environment Down to Earth," *Harvard Business Review* 77, no. 4 (July-August 1999): pp. 149–157, accessed January 25, 2021, https://hbr.org/1999/07/bringing-the-environment-down-to-earth.

8   VW's emission cheating scandal has been widely reported in the media, e.g., see Jack Ewing, "Engineering a Deception: What Led to Volkswagen's Diesel Scandal," *The New York Times*, last modified March 16, 2017, accessed January 25, 2021, www.nytimes.com/interactive/2017/business/

volkswagen-diesel-emissions-timeline.html; or Guilbert Gates et al., "How Volkswagen's 'Defeat Devices' Worked," *The New York Times*, last modified March 16, 2017, accessed January 25, 2021, www.nytimes.com/ interactive/2015/business/international/vw-diesel-emissions-scandal-explained.html.

9   "Solar Is Now 'Cheapest Electricity in History', Confirms IEA," *Carbon Brief*, last modified October 13, 2020, accessed January 3, 2021, www.carbonbrief.org/solar-is-now-cheapest-electricity-in-history-confirms-iea.

10 Clifford Krauss, " 'Is Exxon a Survivor?' The Oil Giant Is at a Crossroads," *The New York Times*, last modified December 10, 2020, accessed January 3, 2021, www.nytimes.com/2020/12/10/business/energy-environment/exxon-mobil-pandemic-energy-transition.html.
    Clifford Krauss, "Exxon Mobil Lost $22 Billion in 2020, Its Worst Performance in Four Decades," *The New York Times*, last modified February 2, 2021, accessed February 2, 2021, www.nytimes.com/live/2021/02/02/business/stock-market-today#exxon-mobil-lost-22-billion-in-2020-its-worst-performance-in-four-decades.

11 Brian Wang, "White LED Lights with 135 Lumens per Watt About Ten Times Better Than Incandescent," *Next Big Future*, last modified August 31, 2010, accessed January 3, 2021, www.nextbigfuture.com/2010/08/white-led-lights-with-135-lumens-per.html.

12 "Ecoinvent Database," *Ecoinvent*, accessed January 25, 2021, www.ecoinvent.org/.

13 "The Higg Materials Sustainability Index," *Sustainable Apparel Coalition*, accessed January 25, 2021, https://apparelcoalition.org/higg-product-tools/.

12

NET GREEN FOR HOUSEHOLDS

In the previous chapter, we defined the role of business as providing the goods and services that people need or want. We can actually trace this idea all the way back to the birth of economics as its own discipline.[1] In 1776, Adam Smith wrote in his book *The Wealth of Nations* that "consumption is the sole end and purpose of all production." Despite this observation, for the next hundred years, economics was preoccupied with advancing the theory of production. Then, in 1871, William Stanley Jevons stated in his book *The Theory of Political Economy* that "the theory of economics must begin with a correct theory of consumption." In his seminal book from 1890, *Principles of Economics*, Alfred Marshall agreed and added that the consumer is the "ultimate regulator of all demands."

In other words, a theory of consumption is required to understand what and how much is being produced. Unfortunately, economics still has no satisfying theory of consumption. The one which emerged in the 19th century and is prevailing to this day is called rational choice. It asserts that consumers make decisions by consistently choosing the most preferred

DOI:10.4324/9781003163060-12

available option based on consistent criteria. The problem of defining 'preferred' is solved by postulating the existence of a quantity called utility. As a result, consumers make rational choices by maximizing their utility, given budget, availability, and other constraints. Throw in the assumption that utility is only derived from self-interest and you have the famous 'homo economicus', which I personally find quite depressing.

A series of tweaks followed to address the many contradictions between this theory and observed behavior. So now consumers have bounded rationality and maximize expected utility. One corollary of using utility maximization as theory of consumption is that the current consumption bundle of households must already be close to optimal. This does not leave much room for changes in consumption. Another side effect is that consuming more is always better, unless something has a negative marginal utility. If the consumer psyche is hard-wired to 'more is better', reduced consumption movements like 'voluntary simplicity' become a bit of a hard sell.

In the late 1990s, I spent some time banging my head against rational choice and expected utility theory. It's sort of a branch of mathematics and more concerned with proving abstract theorems than matching theories with observations. However many proofs I struggled through, I just couldn't shake the feeling that consumers, myself included, simply did not behave in these rigorous mathematical ways. As a result, the utility modeling I did at INSEAD felt phony. I wish I had known back then that psychologists Daniel Kahneman and Amos Tversky had been undoing rational choice and expected utility theory since the late 1970s.[2] They did this so irrefutably that their work was awarded the Nobel Memorial Prize in Economics in 2002. Today, the work of Tversky and Kahneman, together with that of others like Herbert Simon and Richard Thaler, is called behavioral economics.[3] While it constitutes a big improvement, it has been criticized as being a laundry list of biases and decision heuristics rather than a unified theory of behavior.

In a curious parallel to economics, industrial ecology also spent its first decades focusing on the environmental impact of production before discovering the importance of consumption for the pursuit of sustainability. And just like economics currently has no satisfying theory of consumption, there is no real theory of sustainable consumption in industrial ecology.[4] The best we have for the moment are lists of proposed changes in behavior or consumption. Sometimes these suggested changes are ranked by estimated size of the environmental impact reductions, which is almost always measured in GHGs.[5]

If households truly are the 'ultimate regulator of all demands', they do play a critically important role in our project of dramatic environmental impact reduction. And if consumers are not just rigid utility maximizers, whose consumption bundles are already optimized and thus more or less fixed, the project of greening household consumption becomes a lot more viable. In fact, if current consumption bundles and patterns are not necessarily optimal, then greening household consumption might actually increase well-being rather than reduce it.[6]

While there is no doubt that consumer preferences impact and constrain what companies can produce and sell, this should not be used as an excuse for inaction by businesses. When challenged to offer greener products and services, some business managers and spokespersons are all too keen to claim that they have no choice but to provide what consumers demand. Yet, the amount of money that said companies spend on advertising and marketing every year makes such statements of self-absolution sound a little disingenuous. Clearly, influence is exerted in both directions and not just from the consumer to the producer.

In whatever way households arrive at the purchasing decisions they make, the purpose of these purchases is to provide for the members of the household. The role of households on a planet in peril is thus to provide for its members while dramatically reducing the environmental impact of doing so.

The net green concept introduced in Chapter 6 is just as relevant for households as it is for businesses. It also works in much the same way as it does for businesses. The objective of a net green analysis is to identify and assess all environmentally significant consequences of a household activity, such as a purchase or a change in behavior. Again, some of these consequences will be decreases in environmental impact, but others may be increases. Some will be quite obvious but others much less so. Some consequences will be fairly certain and thus easily quantifiable, while others will be shrouded in uncertainty. The job of net green is to help households identify those activities that offer large net environmental impact reductions with acceptable uncertainty.

Frequently, environmentally motivated household activities are geared towards reducing a specific type of environmental impact, such a GHG emissions, water use, or toxicity. We learned in Chapter 3 that we need to be aware of trade-offs between environmental concerns. One example was the choice between single-use and reusable diapers, where the material- and thus solid-waste-intensity of single-use diapers has to be traded off against the energy- and water-intensity of reusable diaper washing. We also saw in Chapter 8 that simply switching materials, say from fossil-based plastic to paper or bioplastic, is bound to run into environmental trade-offs. Environmental trade-offs tell us to look harder for true net green solutions. In the case of diapers, this could be to combine the strengths of both designs, i.e. a reusable shell with a single-use liner. In the case of materials, this may just be to consume less material altogether.

There is a significant amount of literature that studies the environmental footprints of households. Most of them quantify household GHG emissions, typically over a calendar year.[7] These studies consistently find that transportation, housing, and food are the largest sources of household GHG emissions. Together they can add up to around three quarters of total household GHGs. These three categories are therefore obvious targets for impact reduction activities. Impact reduction is just another expression for pollution prevention, so we can use the pollution prevention principles from Chapters 7 through 10 to group and examine some of these activities.

Transportation is typically the single largest category of household GHG emissions. Many GHG reduction recommendations therefore aim at changing travel and transportation behavior.[8] The transportation category itself is dominated by household use of cars, which we discussed extensively throughout the chapters. In Chapter 8, we discussed biofuels and light-weight materials as substitution examples with highly uncertain net environmental outcomes, even if we only consider GHG emissions and ignore environmental trade-offs. In Chapter 9, we pointed out that steady increases in engine efficiency over the decades were outweighed by the fact that our cars became bigger and more powerful, while we also keep driving more year over year. A frequent recommendation is thus to switch transportation modes altogether, from cars to bikes, trains, or buses. It is certainly true that those modes have much lower impact on a person-kilometer basis. The net green concept tells us that any change in household travel behavior needs to avoid more environmental impact than it generates. Riding an e-bike instead of a regular bike will actually increase GHG emissions, if only somewhat. The net green thing to do is to ride an e-bike instead of a car. In the same vein, electric vehicles (EVs) are net green only if they displace more impactful transportation modes and behavior.

For many climate zones, heating is another major source of household GHG emissions. Using a heat pump instead of a natural gas furnace or electric resistance heaters is very likely to significantly reduce a household's heating impacts. As I pointed out in Chapter 4, heat pumps are so efficient because they move existing heat rather than having to generate it. While they are less efficient in very cold environments, their designs have improved so much that they are suitable for most climate zones now.

Unless you're already a vegetarian, the dietary adjustment with the highest potential for reducing the GHG footprint of a household is to change the source of protein from animal-based to plant-based. As mentioned in Chapter 8, beef has such a high GHG intensity that even switching just from beef to fish and poultry will reduce household GHG emissions.

EVs still cost more than internal combustion vehicles, and heat pumps are frequently more expensive to buy and install than gas furnaces or electric resistance heaters. However, EVs and heat pumps costs less to operate than their competitors and therefore typically have lower total cost of ownership. Switching to protein sources with lower GHG intensity will also save money, so all three substitution examples come with overall cost savings. This is regarded as something positive since it provides a financial incentive to make these changes in the first place. There is no question that households need incentives to embrace net green purchases and activities. While I don't want to downplay the power of financial incentives, I also hope that environmental impact reduction will increasingly be its own incentive. As we discussed in Chapter 5, cost savings cause an indirect rebound effect that will reduce the environmental effectiveness of the original change. The best way to mitigate this is to either spend the cost savings on products and services with low impact per dollar or to not have any cost savings in the first place.

An environmental household activity that has low or no financial incentives, but is popular nevertheless, is recycling. As we discussed in Chapter 7, throwing our recyclables into the blue bin is just the first step in a whole chain of events necessary for successful recycling. Once collected, the recyclables need to be separated into single material streams and baled. These bales then go to the actual reprocessers that convert the recyclables into secondary materials. Bales may be too contaminated or otherwise unsuitable for reprocessing, so at this stage the material might still end up in landfill or worse. Next, the secondary material needs to be used to make products for which there is real market demand. Once the products with secondary (recycled) content have been sold, recycling could be called an economic success. However, to actually reduce environmental impact and thus be net green, these goods with secondary content need to avoid the production of goods made from all primary materials. As explained in Chapter 7, such displacement is the only source of environmental benefit from recycling and reuse.

As you can see, it is far from certain that throwing recyclables into a recycling bin leads to environmental impact reduction. To make things worse, households have no real control over what happens with the contents of their recycling bins. There is a different way for households to engage in recycling, though. It is to seek out products with recycled content. In other words, in addition to supplying recyclables, households can, and should, create demand for secondary materials. Purchasing goods made with recycled content instead of all new materials is much more likely to displace primary material production and thus truly reduce environmental impact. I have come to the conclusion that this is a more effective way for households to support the circular economy than dutifully filling their recycling bins. The same is true with reuse. Buying secondary products is more effective than giving your old items to charity shops and consignment stores. And again, if shifting your purchases towards repair, secondary products, and recycled content saves you money, make sure you spend it on goods and services with low impact. If it doesn't save you money, feel good about it. Any reverse rebound effect creates additional environmental impact reduction, and you are also creating employment.

Unfortunately, in studies that rank the GHG reduction potentials of household activities, recycling usually shows up towards the bottom of the lists.[9] Many behavioral changes that are high up on these lists, on the other hand, are reductions in consumption. In other words, they belong to the pollution prevention strategy 'less' discussed in Chapter 9. Examples of such GHG reduction strategies are to fly less, to drive less, to have smaller cars, and to have smaller houses. Obviously, such recommendations are geared towards households that fly and drive significant amounts and have bigger cars and houses to begin with. These ranked lists confirm our observation from Chapter 9 that 'less' is the most effective and important of the three pollution prevention strategies. Indirectly, the lists also suggest that wealthier households have higher GHG footprints, and, indeed, the pertinent literature shows that household GHG emissions increase with household income.[10]

This strong relationship between household income and GHG emissions points towards a potential weakness of impact reduction strategies based on reduced consumption. Household income is spent one way or another, and even if some of it is saved, it is done so for future consumption. Therefore, if households reduce their consumption in one spending category or of one particular product, they will end up spending the money elsewhere. In other words, spending less money on flights and driving means spending it otherwise. The actual environmental impact reduction is thus, as always, the difference between the avoided and incurred impacts. To be net green, such shifts in spending pattern require that the avoided impact per dollar is significantly larger than the incurred impact per dollar. Luckily, with flying and driving, this is bound to be the case. However, it is important to keep in mind that many changes in household behavior that sound like reductions in consumption are actually shifts in consumption.

An overall reduction in consumption would actually require a reduction in household income. This could be more desirable than it may sound. If it also means less work time and more free time, and more free time is valued highly by the household members, then a shift from income to spare time might actually be an attractive option. Indeed, companies all over the world have started to experiment with 4-day workweeks.[11]

If trading income for time isn't for you, then my suggestion is to shift your spending from stuff and other impactful activities to labor. As discussed in Chapter 10, pure labor is as close as it gets to an activity with no environmental impact, so shifting household spending towards labor is always net green. In the previous chapter, I mentioned haircuts, music lessons, exercise classes, and massages as truly green ways to make and spend money, but obviously the list goes on. Labor is also the key ingredient to making maintenance, repair, and reuse possible and net green. Labor could also be regarded as the ultimate substitution strategy and our best bet to truly decouple income from environmental impact. And let's remind ourselves that shifting our spending from stuff to labor furthers not just environmental but also social sustainability goals.

Applying the net green concept to households provides the major insight that households typically shift rather than reduce their consumption. This implies that the typical approach to sustainable consumption, which considers one purchasing decision at a time, is incomplete at best and, in the worst case, even misleading. As we explored throughout this book, purchasing the product alternative with the lower environmental footprint may not be net green if it is also the cheapest option. This means that the current practice of comparing the environmental footprints of alternative products providing equivalent or similar services is not enough for net green decision making. Assuming that households make all their purchasing decisions by choosing from a set of equivalent products or services is also naïve and unrealistic. Once we have taken care of our necessities, we can spend our money as we please, which is why it's called discretionary spending. This leaves a lot of leeway for shifting household spending between categories. A better way to green households might therefore be to consider how changes and shifts in total spending impact their overall environmental footprint. This different view of sustainable consumption would also mean that environmental impact per dollar is a better metric than environmental impact per type of product or service. Such an environmental indicator is also better suited to identify and avoid undesirable rebound effects.

I would like to finish this chapter and, in fact, the entire book with an analogy I found, many years ago, in the corporate sustainability report of the British home improvement retailer B&Q. In this report, B&Q's first Director of Sustainability, Alan Knight, likened sustainability to being a good neighbor. Even though I lost the report in one of my moves, the image stayed with me throughout these years. A good neighbor does not just look after the members of the household but also cares about his or her neighbors and the entire neighborhood. You don't have to be an altruist to see why this is not just the right but also the smart thing to do. Bad neighborly relationships and a neglected neighborhood are a recipe for an unhappy life.

Today, due to our global supply chains, global environmental challenges, global travel, and global media, we live in a world where we are all neighbors to each other. At this point, we are so connected with each other that the entire world is our neighborhood. The idea that we could somehow isolate ourselves from the social struggles and environmental degradation in the rest of the world is becoming increasingly untenable. I believe that the social and environmental upheavals caused by a rapidly changing climate everywhere in the world in recent years have been bringing this message home to a large and growing part of the world's population.

For a household to just look after its members while ignoring the environmental and broader social consequences of its actions and purchases is just not sustainable anymore. It is also a recipe for an unhappy life. In other words, the role of a household on this planet in peril is not just to provide for all household members but also for everyone and everything else. I firmly believe that such a homo sustinens is a better model of human nature than the aforementioned homo economicus.[12]

Notes

1   Frank Trentmann, "How Humans Became 'Consumers': A History," *The Atlantic*, last modified November 28, 2016, accessed January 26, 2021, www.theatlantic.com/business/archive/2016/11/how-humans-became-consumers/508700/.

2   Daniel Kahneman and Amos Tversky, "Prospect Theory: An Analysis of Decision Under Risk," *Econometrica* 47, no. 2 (March 1979): pp. 263–292, accessed January 26, 2021, www.jstor.org/stable/1914185; See also: Michael Lewis, *The Undoing Project: A Friendship That Changed Our Minds* (New York: W. W. Norton & Company, 2016).

3   Justin Fox, "From 'Economic Man' to Behavioral Economics," *Harvard Business Review* 93, no. 5 (May 2015): pp. 78–85, accessed January 26, 2021, https://hbr.org/2015/05/from-economic-man-to-behavioral-economics.

4   Felix Creutzig et al., "Towards Demand-Side Solutions for Mitigating Climate Change," *Nature Climate Change* 8 (2018): pp. 260–263, accessed January 26, 2021, www.nature.com/articles/s41558-018-0121-1.

5   Seth Wynes and Kimberly A. Nichols, "The Climate Mitigation Gap: Education and Government Recommendations Miss the Most Effective Individual Actions," *Environmental Research Letters* 12, no. 7 (2017): p. 074024, accessed January 26, 2021, https://doi.org/10.1088/1748-9326/aa7541.

6   Tim Jackson, "Living Better by Consuming Less?," *Journal of Industrial Ecology* 9, nos. 1–2 (February 2008): pp. 19–36, accessed January 26, 2021, https://doi.org/10.1162/1088198054084734.

7   Angela Druckman and Tim Jackson, "Understanding Households as Drivers of Carbon Emissions," in *Taking Stock of Industrial Ecology*, Roland Clift

and Angela Druckman (Eds.) (Berlin, Germany: Springer, 2016), pp. 181–203, https://link.springer.com/chapter/10.1007/978-3-319-20571-7_9.

8   Diana Ivanova et al., "Quantifying the Potential for Climate Change Mitigation of Consumption Options," *Environmental Research Letters* 15 (2020): p. 093001, accessed January 26, 2021, https://iopscience.iop.org/article/10.1088/1748-9326/ab8589.

9   Diana Ivanova et al., "Quantifying the Potential for Climate Change Mitigation of Consumption Options," *Environmental Research Letters* 15 (2020): p. 093001, accessed January 26, 2021, https://iopscience.iop.org/article/10.1088/1748-9326/ab8589.

10   Angela Druckman and Tim Jackson, "Understanding Households as Drivers of Carbon Emissions," in *Taking Stock of Industrial Ecology*, Roland Clift and Angela Druckman (Eds.) (Berlin, Germany: Springer, 2016), pp. 181–203, https://link.springer.com/chapter/10.1007/978-3-319-20571-7_9.

11   Yuki Noguchi, "Enjoy the Extra Day off! More Bosses Give 4-Day Workweek a Try," *National Public Radio*, last modified February 21, 2020, accessed January 26, 2021, www.npr.org/2020/02/21/807133509/enjoy-the-extra-day-off-more-bosses-give-4-day-workweek-a-try.

12   Bernd Siebenhüner, "*Homo sustinens* – Towards a New Conception of Humans for the Science of Sustainability," *Ecological Economics* 32, no. 1 (2000): pp. 15–25, accessed January 26, 2021, https://doi.org/10.1016/S0921-8009(99)00111-1.

INDEX

Note: Page numbers in italics indicate a figure and page numbers in bold indicate a table on the corresponding page.